Praise for *Traditional Wicca*

"*Traditional Wicca* is a unique and important book. It's amazing to me that in over seventy years of publishing on the subject of Wicca, nothing like this book has ever been written! I'm kind of jealous I didn't think to write it myself. The chapter on initiation is, by itself, worth the cover price. If you want to understand what people mean by 'traditional Wicca,' whether or not you're seeking it, this is the one book you must read."

—Deborah Lipp, Wiccan high priestess
and author of *Merry Meet Again*

"Like the bristles of a besom, Thorn Mooney's *Traditional Wicca* sweeps through the subject of Witchcraft, removing the dust and dirt of ignorance and prejudice to reveal the true heart of Wicca. Thorn writes with obvious sincerity, with feeling, and from experience. Her book covers everything from defining Witchcraft, through the workings of a coven, to actual initiation and beyond. She warns that Wicca is not for everyone and—I am personally delighted to see—includes a chapter on recognizing 'red flags' when first contacting others … especially those who might claim to be more than they actually are. This book is the quintessential guide for the true, sincere seeker."

—Raymond Buckland, author of
Buckland's Complete Book of Witchcraft

"Traditional Wicca is a topic that few actually understand despite its long and distinguished history. With passion and skill, Thorn delivers a book that many familiar with Wicca will wish they had had when they were studying it and those who find themselves on the path for the first time will rejoice at having found. Whether you intend to seek initiation or not, this book is full of valuable gems that will enhance any practice at any level. *Traditional Wicca* is an all-inclusive

tour through the history, practices, and lore of traditional Wicca that weaves voices from all over the tradition and challenges everything you think you know about it."

—Devin Hunter, author of *The Witch's Book of Power*

"A masterful gem of insight and wisdom, *Traditional Wicca* reveals the time-honored practices of initiatory Wicca, thought all but lost by many, but hidden like so many occult secrets in plain sight. Drawing a clear and respectful distinction between eclectic Wicca and its older, more traditional sibling, Thorn Mooney takes us on a personal journey exploring the powers and the pitfalls of the initiatory inner court, revealing the persistence of a thriving and dynamic Craft that is at once orthopraxic and changing, traditional and experimental. With practical advice for the seeker, peppered with personal anecdotes from several practitioners and initiates alike, this book is a much-needed map … Highly recommended."

—Storm Faerywolf, author of *Betwixt and Between*

TRADITIONAL
WICCA

About the Author

Thorn Mooney is a Witch of more than twenty years and the high priest-ess of Foxfire, a traditional Gardnerian coven thriving in the American South. She holds a graduate degree in religious studies and has worked as a university lecturer, public school teacher, tarot reader, writer, and musician. Thorn maintains the blog *Oathbound* for Patheos Pagan and writes a regular column for *Witches & Pagans* magazine. Aside from her esoteric pursuits, Thorn is a competitive historical fencer and HEMA practitioner, a traditional archer, and a seasoned guitarist. She lives in Charlotte, North Carolina. Visit her and find more of her work at www.thornthewitch.com.

TRADITIONAL WICCA

A Seeker's Guide

THORN MOONEY

Llewellyn Publications
Woodbury, Minnesota

FIRST EDITION
Sixth Printing, 2024

Book design by Donna Burch-Brown
Cover illustration by Jennifer Hewitson
Cover design by Shira Atakpu
Interior art by Jennifer Hewitson

Llewellyn Publications is a registered trademark of Llewellyn Worldwide Ltd.

Library of Congress Cataloging-in-Publication Data
https://lccn.loc.gov/2018009920
ISBN: 978-0-7387-5359-1

Llewellyn Worldwide Ltd. does not participate in, endorse, or have any authority or responsibility concerning private business transactions between our authors and the public.

All mail addressed to the author is forwarded but the publisher cannot, unless specifically instructed by the author, give out an address or phone number.

Any internet references contained in this work are current at publication time, but the publisher cannot guarantee that a specific location will continue to be maintained. Please refer to the publisher's website for links to authors' websites and other sources.

Llewellyn Publications
A Division of Llewellyn Worldwide Ltd.
2143 Wooddale Drive
Woodbury, MN 55125-2989
www.llewellyn.com

Printed in the United States of America

For Gwynn

Contents

Acknowledgments

A book is sort of like a snapshot. It's just one image, plucked from a whole life. And just like how a photograph can only really show you that one moment, a book can usually only leave us with conjectures about what was behind it—the events and people that impacted its creation. A lot happened to me while I was writing this, and a lot of people helped me write it, even if they didn't know that's what they were doing.

To Gwynn. You asked me what you'd done to deserve my dedication. You answered the phone late at night and grounded me with your humor, giving me someplace to go when I felt completely unmoored. You loved me anyway. I would not have been able to do any of this without you.

To Lady Epona, Autumn Moon, Foxfire, and the Coven de la Unicorn family. Thank you for this ridiculously magical life.

To Corvus and Lore. Thank you for putting up with me while I was writing this book and for being the real magic behind Foxfire Coven. We wouldn't be a thing without you two. Extra special thanks to your mom.

To Lukaos, because you jumped ship with me and somehow neither one of us has drowned yet.

To the rowdy pack of coyotes that keeps showing up to my living room for circle. Thank you for the laughter, for the honesty, and for keeping me from running too far into the woods.

To my sword family, for inviting me in (and then letting me stay), for keeping me grounded, challenging me, and making sure that there's always a glass of wine within reach. I don't have words for how much I love you, which is probably the real reason I hit too hard.

Finally, to Jason Mankey, for making me feel like maybe I could be a writer. You guys should all go read his books and buy him cider and whiskey everywhere he goes for being so awesome.

Wherever we all are once this moment has passed, and whatever snapshots we leave behind, you have my love.

INTRODUCTION

It's finally sunset.

Candles flicker in their holders, nestled amongst the damp leaves strewn at the edges of the circle. Up the lip of the embankment, through the poplars and oaks, you can still hear the city. Motors and sirens hum distantly, melding into a single tone, counterpoint to the chirruping insects and the fluttering bats, awakened with the darkness. This is only a wooded cluster, set between the asphalt and streetlamps and brick buildings of human industry. It is easy for the careless to overlook, despite its central location. Of the city, yet not. Betwixt and between.

A good place for magic.

The leaves have been carefully swept, revealing dark earth and twisted roots. There is a low, round altar positioned at the circle's center, and twin candles cast shadows across mysterious objects. Coils of slender rope, like snakes. The glint of steel, like twinkling eyes. The reflective surface of a dish filled with water. Shadowy icons fashioned in clay that seem to swell with the flickering light, evoking a sense of timelessness. This is something both new and ancient. Alluring and frightening. Surprising and yet completely familiar and welcoming.

Robed figures move amongst the trees and then into the light of the circle, surrounding the altar. Several moments of silence pass between them as they feel the weight of this place and settle into its rhythms. Suddenly, with only a shared look, they allow the fabric to unfold and drop from their bodies. Glittering firelight trails across bare skin, warm despite the night chill. They begin to move in sync, and a low chant erupts, calling to the powers of this place. The sound vibrates an invocation to the gods of the Wica, reaching back in time across generations, a thread of shared power passed from circle to circle.

We're finally home.

Me, Foxfire, and the Witch Cult

A lot can happen in twenty years. The Wicca I practice today isn't the same Wicca I was studying when I picked up my first book, surfed to my first America Online chat room, or created my first profile on the Witches' Voice.[1] I was a young teenager, caught up in something that felt magical and true. It felt like something that could change my life, and it did, though that change was gradual and intermingled with all the other profound changes that go along with becoming an adult. At sixteen—having gorged myself on every book by Silver RavenWolf and Scott Cunningham—I felt like I knew everything about the Craft there was to know. I did what a lot of young people do and set myself up as a guide for others. I lectured other teenagers in online forums. I insisted that I must be an "old soul." I handed out advice freely, whether it was solicited or not. Yeah, I was pretty arrogant (imagine a less reflective, more self-righteous first-year Hermione Granger). I even started writing a book, typing furiously on my dad's old laptop. It was to be an introductory book on Wicca—my own self-important response to Silver RavenWolf's *Teen Witch*, written by a teen. I worked hard and I wrote more than 20,000 words before college got in the way.

Of course, it was also around that time that I began to come slowly to the realization that, in fact, I did not know everything there was to know about Wicca. I discovered eBay and acquired my first cop-

---

1. The Witches' Voice, www.witchvox.com, has been around since 1997 and remains an important resource, though many have moved on to other web platforms.

ies of Gerald Gardner's *Witchcraft Today* and *The Meaning of Witchcraft*. They were dense and convoluted and foreign. I didn't recognize my Wicca here, though these books still felt important. This wasn't just candles in my bedroom and a never-ending parade of lackluster drum circles and public rituals. *This was a secret Witch cult.* I also met other Wiccans for the first time—people who had been at this longer and did things differently from me. I read more and read books that hadn't been available to me before. I no longer felt qualified to write that book or to solicit those questions from newbies online. It was uncomfortable, but also exciting. It's easy to feel bored when you think you know everything.

I grew up slowly, reading and experimenting along the way. Eventually—once I knew for sure that there was more than what was in the books, which had started to feel like the same book over and over again—I sought out a teacher and a coven. That process wasn't easy. There were a lot of false starts, a lot of disappointments, and a lot of late nights spent wondering what I was doing. But all that taught me so much more than what I could have imagined at sixteen, in my adolescent arrogance. Once I gave up the assumption that I already knew what Wicca was and what it had to offer, my real education began.

Today, I'm the high priestess of a coven in the Gardnerian tradition of Wicca. That coven, Foxfire, is the product of a lot of hard work— a lot of tears and a lot of magic. Most of my life revolves around my practice of the Craft: training students, organizing circles, practicing magic, conducting research into our history, exploring other kinds of Witchcraft, and, as always, writing. I've been blogging about my own involvement in Wicca for more than ten years. I finished a graduate degree in religious studies at a major university. I've presented my academic work on Witchcraft at national, scholarly conferences. I've published articles, made YouTube videos, taught workshops at Pagan festivals, and befriended all kinds of Witches and Pagans along the way. I learn best by observing others and listening to their stories, so

I've tried to make my own available to whoever might benefit from them. That includes my failures, my mistakes, and my doubts, which have been just as important to me as my successes. In turn, I like to stay involved with a lot of different kinds of Witch communities, and I've seen a lot happen over the decades.

Like I said, a lot can change in twenty years!

How to Use This Book

I'm writing now because much of what I hear, read, and see in current conversations about Wicca—online, in new books, and out in Witchcraft communities—reminds me of my own teenaged assumptions. The heyday of solitary, eclectic, do-it-yourself Wicca seems to be over. Our Pagan communities aren't just bigger; they're also more diverse and complex. Wicca is often still the entry point for many new Pagans and Witches, but there's so much more available and so much more easily accessed. People move on from Wicca sooner, or they never consider it to begin with. Sometimes, this is genuinely because they belong elsewhere—Wicca is not and has never been for everyone—but other times it's because they assume that Wicca is fundamentally lacking: lacking depth, lacking longevity, lacking relevance, or lacking self-reflection. Had I stopped where I was as a teenager—assuming that I knew everything and had seen it all—I probably would have come to agree and left myself.

But in seeking a traditional Wiccan coven, I learned that the Wicca I'd studied in books wasn't the full picture. Maybe it wasn't part of the same picture at all. And the Wicca I came to love wasn't even included in most treatments of Wicca or popular discussions. Everyone seemed to think the traditional covens were gone, or else they never knew about them to begin with. What had once been the dominant strain of contemporary Witchcraft seemed to be slowly disappearing. When other Witches and Pagans spoke about Wicca (especially when they spoke disparagingly), I didn't recognize the Wicca they would describe. I heard a lot about how Wiccans are wishy-washy, just taking whatever gods they like from whatever culture without putting any care into it. I'm periodically lectured about how Wiccans often don't practice magic and never practice baneful or defensive magic (news to me!). It's even become trendy to insist that we're not practicing Witchcraft at all—just a gentle blend of New Age healing techniques and feel-good self-therapy. Wiccans are shallow. Wicca only appeals to teen girls (and, hey, have you ever noticed how, as a culture, we're so often dismissive of the things that young women love?). Wicca is "beginner" Paganism. Wicca isn't relevant anymore. Wicca is Witchcraft declawed.

In conversations about "real" Witchcraft, I've increasingly found that Wiccans are no longer included. Partially, this is reflective of the need to make space for other voices and other traditions. It's absolutely true that certain kinds of Wicca have dominated Pagan spaces, drowning out others. It's true that many newcomers approach Witchcraft and assume that Wicca is all there is, so they misunderstand members of other traditions. It's also true that some Wiccans are assholes. I think that's true of some people in every group.

But the loudest, most circulated voices are not necessarily the most representative. The Wicca that you see on bookshelves, in internet memes, and at open circles isn't all there is. And the sad state of things is that, because everyone already seems to think they know all there is, there are very few resources for those who are curious about traditional Wicca (at least, resources that are less than twenty years old). It's hard to suss out other perspectives, hear real stories from contemporary practitioners, and learn how to become involved, if that's something you aspire to do.

This book is not necessarily intended to sell you on traditional Wicca. I believe that sincere, dedicated seekers will still find their way, without the need for prodding or proselytizing. There's also a whole world of incredible Witchcraft and Pagan traditions that are worth exploring. Rather, this book is designed as a resource for those who are already in the process of seeking. Seeking is tough, and most of the published guidance available is outdated. It can be hard to know where to turn. It may also benefit readers who are simply curious about older forms of Wicca or critics who may be wondering if Wicca has anything to offer beyond the popular forms detailed in the last twenty years of introductory books.

Here, you'll find practical advice for seeking, both from me and from a number of other traditional Wiccans at various stages in their practice. Look for their input in the sections labeled "From the Circle." You'll learn how to recognize healthy, reputable covens and avoid the duds. You'll learn how to navigate the process of asking for training and how to succeed in an outer court. You'll also get advice on what to do if you can't find a coven, aren't yet old enough to be a seeker, or just can't set aside the time for training at this time in your life. We'll talk frankly about some of those controversial issues: initiation, hierarchy, nudity, sex, and cursing.

I want to invite you to consider that you know less about Wicca than you think you do. If your hunch is that Wicca is more than what you've been told—deeper than what you've read and more profound than what you may have experienced through open rituals or Pagan Pride Day festivities—then I'm here to confirm your suspicions. You're right.

PART I
MEETING
THE WICA

A DIFFERENT SORT OF WICCA

People come to traditional Wicca for a variety of reasons. Some are looking for a teacher within an established system that already has protocol and techniques for helping newcomers become effective magical practitioners. For some, it's just easier to learn when you've got others in place to guide you. Others are interested in connecting with and becoming part of an established history. There's something powerful about feeling like you're part of something bigger and older than you. Many—because of their personalities or prior experience in similarly structured religions—enjoy a more hierarchical, ordered approach. Structures and expectations that may feel confining to some are actually beneficial to others. Finally, seekers to traditional Wicca may be mostly interested in the opportunity to work in a coven setting, which is an option that tends to be a little less available in other forms of Wicca.

Why Traditional Wicca?

There's definitely something to be said for joining an established tradition, particularly one with a history that spans several decades. It's a little like marrying into a big family. You'll find that, in addition to your own coven, you'll have connections to others. Sometimes this extended family network can be quite far-flung. There are Gardnerians, for example, all over the world. When I travel—particularly in the United States or Europe—I often check to see if I'll have Craft family nearby. If I'm lucky, I'll have the opportunity to visit, exchange stories, share meals, and otherwise enjoy the company of Witches who share core elements of practice, as well as a common history. It's like having built-in friends everywhere you go! It's an amazing feeling when you know that you're connected to so many others whom you may not otherwise ever meet.

As a member of a tradition, you'll also enjoy the benefits of knowing that Craft practice and lore doesn't end with the people leading your own coven. You may find that your Craft education comes through other sources—maybe the Witches who trained your own leaders, texts left by Witches who have died, or through the contacts you'll make in "sister" covens. When my own high priestess or high priest doesn't have an answer to one of my questions, they can refer me to someone who does. That sort of communal access to lore is a rare and precious thing. To some extent, this is what others may be able to accomplish through reading books and conducting research, but the traditionalist has the advantage of more sources, and usually with considerably less legwork. In traditional Craft, your elders are there specifically to aid you. Solitary practitioners usually aren't so lucky.

And, of course, this network of elders (and siblings and cousins…) isn't just practical. It's also magical! Your initiatory lineage represents a transfer of occult power that, at least in theory, gives you a magical advantage over other kinds of practitioners. Obviously, this cannot be taken as assured, nor is it meant to be a sweeping statement, but at the very least you become connected to a magical source that represents a kind of power (even if it's purely emotional) beyond just what you could do alone. Your magical tools and techniques are reinforced by the power of earlier generations of Witches. Every circle you stand in connects you to every circle cast before. The weight of the power within your tradition goes beyond just yourself. Instead, you may tap into an egregore—a kind of magical group mind—that spans generations.

On a more practical level, some people simply learn and function more effectively in structured environments. Most of us learned to read and write within established school curricula, guided by an experienced teacher who had received particular training, supported by time-proven educational theory. This doesn't work for everyone—the system isn't perfect—but usually, you can't simply leave a small child with books and expect that she'll naturally become a fluent reader. She'll need assistance from someone with a specific skill set.

Traditional Wicca operates under similar assumptions. Some people are perfectly happy to read books, surf the internet, and teach themselves through trial and error. But many others benefit from a learning environment that includes structure, modeling from more adept practitioners, and feedback from peers and teachers (which is probably how you learned to read and perform arithmetic). Even as a solitary, you're still at least partially relying on similar strategies (with books as your teachers and feedback coming from friends or online contacts, for example). A traditional coven simply formalizes this process. Like in school, you may be asked to read particular books, complete set assignments, or perform particular tasks. If not that, you will at least be asked to learn through observation, discussion, and guided practice. This sort of facilitated learning ensures steady progress, more thorough understanding, and greater consistency in outcome (i.e., more effective magical practice, more qualified future coven leaders, etc.).

This analogy between traditional coven work and school should be understood loosely. Your experience probably won't actually *feel* like school. Rather, I want to emphasize that their underlying structures are similar: there will be more experienced practitioners guiding less experienced practitioners according to pre-established ideas about what is important and most effective. Beyond that, individual covens (even in the same tradition) may vary dramatically. I know some covens that require essays and research papers and others that expect students to learn primarily through listening and observing. There is a spectrum of possibilities here.

This leads to another important point. Just like school, traditional covens tend to be hierarchical. This means that there are leaders in place to instruct less experienced members, who may or may not have much say in how the coven operates. Underneath these leaders (usually a high priestess, a high priest, or both) there may be other official roles that determine additional hierarchy. Often, this manifests in the form of a degree system, with levels of experience and ability marked by first, second, and third degree ranks. Depending on the coven, there may be additional positions (such as summoner or maiden). Even before you're initiated, you will likely find yourself in a type of training group called an outer court, which allows you to explore the coven's ritual structure, beliefs, and the unique personalities of coven members and leaders before formally committing to membership. As the most inexperienced in the tradition (if not in Witchcraft as a whole), these students may receive guidance from initiates at any degree level.

Hierarchy can make some people uncomfortable. Pagans in particular tend to be highly individualistic, especially if they come from religious backgrounds that have felt structurally oppressive or constraining. Many people are initially attracted to Wicca *because* of its apparent lack of boundaries. The idea that you might need to submit to the demands of a high priestess or some other grand poobah isn't just unappealing, it's downright offensive. This position is understandable, especially for people who've suffered under abusive power regimes. This is often a key factor in the decision of whether or not to pursue a traditional Wiccan path. In part 2 of this book, there's a whole chapter on hierarchy in traditional Wicca and how and why it works, but this is an important issue so I want to address a few things right away:

The key difference is that coven hierarchy is not intended to be permanent, nor should it ever be arbitrary or abusive. The hierarchy exists to foster growth amongst members. Your high priest shouldn't be collecting first degree initiates just to ensure that he always has someone to pick up his dry cleaning or scrub his bathroom. It's the responsibility of more experienced members to assist less experi-

enced members so that they, too, may one day become high priestesses and high priests in their own right. A schoolteacher has her class
for a period of time, eventually passing her students to someone else
once they've mastered her class content. At some point, those students
should graduate and become adults (and some of them may then
become teachers themselves). This is a type of purposeful hierarchy.
Good teachers do not abuse their students, nor do they keep them
forever. Similarly, good coven leaders teach their initiates to be effective as well as independent. First and second degrees follow the in-
structions of the leading third degree not because she's arbitrarily the
boss, but because she has wisdom and experience beyond their own.
In turn, it is the third degree's job to impart that wisdom and experience to those first and second degrees. This is necessarily an act of
great trust, and it comes with a very heavy responsibility on the part of
those leaders. Abuse can and does happen—just like it does in school
systems and government—but this is not inherent. This is a failure on
the part of those who set themselves up as leaders. It may be the result
of a lack of training, or it may be the result of personality flaws. Being
a Witch doesn't mean someone is automatically a good person. Your
common sense will serve you well in recognizing this sort of dysfunction. If something feels wrong, it probably is.

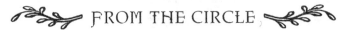 FROM THE CIRCLE

I know nothing about traditional Wicca. I thought I did until I met you and your coven. I thought it was patriarchal,
that it was adverse to creative thinking and full of nonsensical
dogma, because that is what I had been told. I had been told
that Gardnerians were elitist jerks. And then I met a bunch of
amazingly talented, kind people who only ever met my questions with genuineness. Seeing those kinds of people thrive in a
Gardnerian system, it made me realize that many of those no-
tions must be incorrect. You told me at one point that Wicca
provides people with tools to connect with the divine and get

things done. I want to learn how to do that in a reliable way. It turns out I know nothing. But now I want to know everything.

—*Acacia, outer court member,*
excerpted from an initial inquiry to Foxfire Coven

What Is Traditional Wicca?

So what exactly is traditional Wicca, and what distinguishes it from other kinds of Wicca and Witchcraft? These are deceptively complex questions. Whole academic texts have been devoted to discussions of the word "traditional" and many more on what constitutes Witchcraft and whether or not it is necessarily distinct from Wicca.

I wish to acknowledge the complexity of these conversations and emphasize that numerous perspectives exist, complete with vehement opponents. On the one hand, it can feel like a frustrating, petty obsession with semantics. Who cares what words we use as long as we understand the concepts that they represent? On the other hand, how we use words and how we assign them meaning has very real consequence in the world. Historically, who falls under the category of "Witch" has been a matter of life and death. Where matters of religion are at stake—and Witchcraft is a matter of religion for many—conversations tend to become particularly heated. Our words matter, and we should use them with care while at the same time understanding that words may carry multiple meanings and rarely belong to only one group of people.

In this book, I seek to be as inclusive as possible, allowing readers to interpret these categories as best suits them. I've tried to choose language that reflects common usage while acknowledging divergence where appropriate. I will fail sometimes, and I apologize in advance. In no case do I mean offense. I tend to see language as being more fluid than static, and the terms I've chosen (as well as how I've defined them) are designed to familiarize readers with wider trends, not to persuade them that my way is the only way. When in doubt, it's always fair to simply ask someone what they mean.

I tend to use "Wicca" and "Witchcraft" interchangeably. I do this because "Wicca" literally means "Witch," and the earliest forms of Wicca were understood to be a kind of Witchcraft. However, at no point in these early days (way back in the mid-twentieth century) was Wicca widely understood to be the *only* kind of Witchcraft, nor should it be now. There are many kinds of Witches in the world, and only some of them are Wiccan. Further, today there is a growing faction of Wiccans who do not consider themselves to be Witches, either because they do not feel that they are really practicing Witchcraft (which is usually defined as a particular kind of magic) or because they wish to divorce their practices from a term that has historically carried a lot of negativity. In either case, Wiccans tend to define themselves as practitioners of a particular religion, the characteristics of which we'll discuss in detail shortly.

Witchcraft, more broadly, is frequently described as a "practice" rather than a religion in and of itself. This sort of distinction raises complex questions about what a "religion" is (again, more than a few academic texts have been produced across centuries wrestling with these issues), but generally we should know that while some Witches (and Wiccans especially) see their Witchcraft as necessarily tied to a spiritual practice, others see it as purely "craft," which may be combined with religion or may be employed from a secular perspective. For this reason, the word "Witchcraft" may be capitalized or not, depending on who is doing the writing (in this book, I've chosen to capitalize to avoid the confusion of alternating cases depending on which kind of Craft I'm discussing). All of this is very much up to the individual Witch, and I usually recommend avoiding sweeping generalizations like, "All Witches believe…" or "All Wiccans practice X while all Witches practice Y." There will always be someone standing by to prove you wrong.

My decision to use "Wicca" and "Witchcraft" interchangeably was largely a matter of convenience. Also, it reflects an attitude prevalent amongst traditional Wiccans that Wicca is fundamentally a kind of

Witchcraft, and that all Wiccans are Witches. Other kinds of practitioners hold different opinions—and these may be worth considering—but historically and popularly, these terms have long been used in this way and still are in most traditional circles.

In order to define traditional Wicca and to distinguish it from the other kinds of Wicca and Witchcraft you've probably read about, we should begin by considering its origins. Wicca is a religious movement that developed in the mid-twentieth century thanks primarily to the efforts of British civil servant Gerald Brosseau Gardner. Gardner, who was heavily influenced by and interested in folklore, magic, and his own travels in Asia, was interested in reviving what he saw as the indigenous religion of Britain. Carefully (and sometimes not so carefully), he assembled the popular anthropology of the day, along with his own explorations and personal experience, into a coherent system that he believed was true to an ancient practice of religious Witchcraft. Drawing from his own background in Freemasonry and his wider studies in other Western magical traditions (including the work of magician Aleister Crowley), Gardner built the scaffolding necessary to support the development and spread of this new (ancient) religion. He didn't do all of this by himself, of course. Gardner claimed to have been initiated into a survival of this ancient "Witch cult" (that was his term, which didn't have the same connotations as today) and was only allowed to reveal it to the public so that it might survive. He built upon these fragments, creating the framework of a contemporary movement. Along the way, he had help assembling and further publishing about and promoting the Witchcraft tradition that would come to be called Wicca. An assortment of subsequent initiates—most prominently Doreen Valiente—contributed material of their own, whether original compositions or pieces from other works of literature and religious liturgy.

This early form of Wicca was initiatory, coven-based, and centered upon a central Mystery surrounding a moon goddess and a horned god of death and hunting. These two deities were variously understood to be universal Witch deities, gods specific to the British Isles, archetypal representations of any or all deities, or little gods of the local people and land.[2]

That's quite a lot of variety! How can a pair of gods be understood so differently while still being part of a coherent tradition? Largely, this is because Gardner's Wicca was experiential—everyone had their own experience of the gods. The tradition was—*is*—particularly concerned with practice over belief. Members are united by a set of ritual practices and a body of rituals, collected in the Book of Shadows (which is a single, specific book, not a personal journal like in other kinds of Wicca), rather than a dogmatic set of beliefs. The details of these rituals are secret, reserved only for initiates. They're closely guarded, but their structure and implements will be familiar to anyone with any casual knowledge of Wicca: a quartered circle, an altar set with a particular assortment of tools, elemental representations, and symbols of the male and female aspects of the divine. The liturgical year fell according to four greater sabbats (with four more eventually added), which marked both the passage of seasons and stages in a repeating myth, in which the goddess and god are central.

This earliest form of Wicca was originally just called the Witch cult, Witchcraft, or, later, "the Wica." Eventually, it came to be called "Gardnerian," after its founder (or promoter, depending on your perspective). The label was actually meant to be disparaging, applied by Robert Cochrane, another Witch who began writing after Gardner, making similar claims of belonging to a surviving Witchcraft tradition.[3] But the name stuck, particularly since this increased openness about Witchcraft meant that other kinds of Witches could also be public. It didn't take long for Gardner's Wicca to split into or simply inspire other kinds of Wicca—both in Europe and in the United States—and, simultaneously, other

---

2. Gerald Gardner, *Witchcraft Today* (New York: Citadel Press, 1954), 31.

3. Robert Cochrane and Evan John Jones, *The Robert Cochrane Letters: An Insight into Modern Traditional Witchcraft*, ed. Michael Howard (Somerset, UK: Capall Bann 2002), 23–24.

kinds of Witchcraft also came to the fore. Some of these other kinds of Witchcraft shared similar language, ritual structure, and origins. Others were more specific to particular regions and held to different mythos. The term "Wicca" was used widely without much of today's care for specific defining boundaries.

These boundaries became somewhat more codified with a boom in publishing and the circulation of information on Witchcraft, particularly in the United States after the 1970s. There were also more initiates, both within Gardnerian Wicca and other forms of Craft (notably Alexandrian and Cochrane's own Clan of Tubal Cain). There were not enough, however, to accommodate the surplus of seekers, whose interest had been piqued by the widening circulation of books and newsletters pertaining to Witchcraft, psychic development, and the occult. Without the availability of coven training—or sometimes in spite of it— interested people began to practice on their own, assembling the rites as best they could, doing their own research into folklore and magic, and writing their own materials through trial and error.

By the end of the twentieth century, a number of prominent books existed to assist would-be Witches in becoming "solitary practitioners," Witches who worked alone and learned primarily through reading. The most influential texts were Raymond Buckland's *Complete Book of Witchcraft* (1986), Scott Cunningham's *Wicca: A Guide for the Solitary Practitioner* (1988), and an assortment of works from Stewart and Janet Farrar. Later, authors such as Silver RavenWolf would further popularize this new form of solitary, do-it-yourself Wicca, which had by now been codified under the moniker "eclectic Wicca" because practitioners could select and use techniques as they saw fit, without being beholden to a particular tradition or teacher.

The sudden availability of these kinds of books, combined with the development of the internet, led to the rise of a huge variety of styles within Wicca (and Witchcraft broadly). Aside from the increase in the number of solitary practitioners (who by now outnumbered Witches in initiatory covens), it became very common to find covens formed according to similar prerogatives. Anyone with desire and access to the right books could become a Wiccan and potentially start their own coven.

As you can imagine, this incredible growth (and variety) created a number of tensions. If Wicca was now available on the internet and at chain bookstores, did people still need formal training and initiation into a lineaged coven? Where would that leave the people still practicing according to Gardner's model? And how much could be changed before this Wicca stopped being Wicca and became some other kind of Witchcraft or Pagan religion? What were the differences, anyway? Did it matter? Many of these newer eclectic covens had never even been exposed to these early forms of Wicca. They focused on different gods and myths, performed different rites, and held different beliefs, particularly emphasizing a moral code now widely called the Wiccan Rede, which was popularized (at least in what people now call "the long version") in the late seventies and eighties thanks to the publication of Gwen Thompson's poem "Rede of the Wiccae" in *Green Egg Magazine* in 1975.[4] Given that there could be so much difference—not excluding what had previously been considered essential to Wiccan practice: an ecstatic passing of power through formal initiation into a supposedly ancient Witch cult—what exactly did it mean to be Wiccan?

There is still quite a lot of debate around this subject, as there invariably is whenever change and schism occur in any group of people. The purpose of this book is not to question the validity of any kind of Wicca, nor is it to assert the correctness of any one tradition or practice. I believe these to be hopeless tasks and would prefer to spend my time actually practicing my own Wicca, regardless of what others may think of it. Instead, I offer my own experience, having participated in a spectrum of Wiccan traditions in both coven and solitary environments. It is my intent here to provide guidance to those who feel

---

4. For a detailed analysis of Rede of the Wicca and additional historical insight, check out *The Rede of the Wiccae: Adriana Porter, Gwen Thompson and the Birth of a Tradition of Witchcraft* by Robert Mathiesen and Theitic (Olympian Press, 2005).

called to pursue that older, more organized form of Wicca, now simply called traditional.

Traditional Wicca, unlike eclectic Wicca, usually traces an initiatory lineage to one of those early Wiccan founders, particularly Gerald Gardner or Alex Sanders. Overwhelmingly, traditional Wicca emphasizes formal training within a coven setting, culminating in initiation and elevation through a degree system. Aside from a shared initiation experience, a shared body of rites or some other common core of practice further unites covens within a tradition. Usually, as in Gardnerian Wicca, this involves the passing of the Book of Shadows or some other body of liturgy or oral lore (and often plenty of both). Theoretically, two initiates from different covens could meet for the first time and find that they connect through this intimate, shared knowledge. This is a profound experience, and it is one of the reasons why seekers are initially attracted to work within an established tradition. Even when, as is common over the course of training, an individual Witch finds herself temporarily separated from her coven, she is still united in praxis. Thus, the traditional Wiccan may be a solitary practitioner without ever really being alone.

Traditional Wicca is also usually marked by higher levels of organization. This should not be taken to mean that traditional covens are stodgy, static, or perform their rites by rote. Rather, it means that particular structures are in place to encourage growth in individual members over time as well as continuity across the tradition as a whole. As in my earlier analogy about school, seekers are brought in and taught by elders, who are usually arranged in a hierarchy. This is not to discourage creativity or independence but rather to facilitate learning and steady, consistent growth. A good teacher need not be draconian. A hierarchy need not be oppressive.

In recent years, a number of eclectic Wiccan systems have organized and expanded to the extent that we might fairly call them traditions in and of themselves, though they may not possess a lineage in the same manner that, for example, Alexandrian or Gardnerian Wicca does. As the years pass and these new traditions continue to survive and grow, they may come to more closely resemble these older Wiccan traditions, but it is reasonable to expect quite a lot of variation in praxis, structure, and protocol. In addition to this general guide, it would be useful to consult any texts that specifically pertain to whatever individual tradition you may be seeking.

For the purposes of this book, I understand traditional Wicca to be:

1. Coven-based

2. Initiatory

3. Lineaged

4. Hierarchical

5. Experiential

Eclectic forms of Wicca may (and often do) include some of these elements. Likewise, individual covens within traditional Wicca may not emphasize all of these criteria equally (though they will usually possess them). We will explore all of these in turn. In part 2, I'll detail each of these five characteristics in individual chapters. In part 3, we'll get down to the practical business of finding and joining a coven, along with the pitfalls to avoid. We'll also tackle some of the issues that arise in wider traditional Wiccan communities and that you'll probably encounter at some point in the course of your seeking or training.

Finally—in one last consideration of semantics—I wish to acknowledge some of the problems that arise from the use of the term "eclectic" to describe systems of Wicca that stand in contrast to traditional Wicca. In Pagan and Witchcraft communities, the description "eclectic" arose in the nineties and early two thousands, popularized by solitary Wiccans and Pagans who had not been formally initiated into one of the established traditions of the day. It meant that these practitioners created, borrowed, or modified materials as needed, usually according to personal interest and through trial and error. It was not by itself a pejorative term, though it became one in many traditional communities.

Today, it is still common for solitary or otherwise self-taught Witches to refer to their practices as eclectic, though as covens and more established systems spring out of the work of these first eclectic practitioners, it becomes more common to see more specific descriptors. Some of these eclectic systems have been around for decades and are really only eclectic in name. They may be just as organized and regulated as any traditional coven from decades past. All this to say that "eclectic" sometimes simply means "not part of an older tradition" rather than that members pick and choose materials or otherwise don't have an established system.

Similarly, "traditional" should not be taken to mean that practitioners never pull from outside sources, don't experiment with new techniques, or don't create their own liturgy. Historically, Wicca develops out of a number of sources and is influenced by a variety of people. Because of this, even the staunchest traditional Wiccan might be fairly described as eclectic.

Use these terms to guide your seeking and to communicate in the various situations you will no doubt find yourself. Do not try to obsessively put every Witch you meet into one category or the other. You'll find yourself very frustrated! At some point, our narrow boxes stop being useful and just start hindering us. Use these terms only as starting points. When they stop being useful, find new ones.

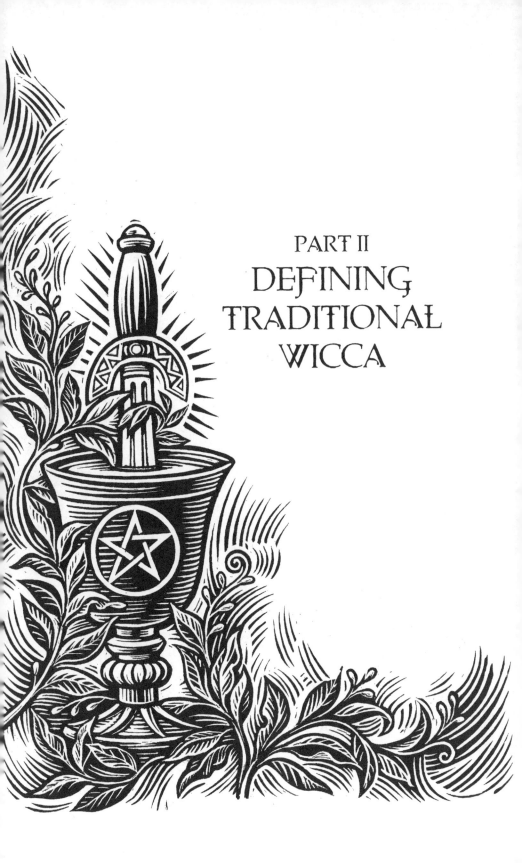

PART II
DEFINING TRADITIONAL WICCA

CHAPTER 2

THE COVEN

The candles are beginning to burn low. Hours after their initial lighting, wax collects in deep puddles and drips down what remains of each shaft, pooling in hardening clumps on the altar top. The scent of frankincense and rose hangs heavy in the air, still vibrating from the power summoned to this place. The energy of the sabbat dance has begun to settle, and seven contented Witches now lounge in sacred space, happily uncorking fresh bottles of wine and passing blessed cakes. The Work done, the circle still strong, it's time to reflect, plan, laugh, and enjoy the company of chosen family.

"Man, I missed you guys." Wren shakes her head and sighs contentedly as she takes the bottle from Eis and pours herself a cup of wine. "I really needed that. Work has just been bogging me down lately. With the holidays coming up, we're really looking to hire somebody in time for next semester, and I feel like all I do is sit in meetings. Plus I'm reading this book on Cerridwen right now, and it's totally messing with my head. I've been having really weird dreams lately."

At the mention of Cerridwen, Corvus snaps to attention, a cookie halfway to her mouth. She read *The Mabinogion* last year, and since then she's felt a powerful affinity for the famous Welsh Witch.

"You need to come to the lake with me! When I started learning about Cerridwen, I had weird dreams, too. There's this lake near my apartment complex, and I started walking down there and actually just trying to talk to her. I don't really know why, but it helps. I feel like I can hear her there."

"That'd be great! I feel like I'm in over my head here." Wren grins, and the two women agree to plan their own magical adventure tomorrow.

"What are we doing for our New Year ritual next month? Do we have plans yet?" Lore interjects.

"Can we go back to that same cemetery? The one Lukaos took us to outside of Asheville? The view from the mountain was amazing in the fog." Corvus leans back on a cushion.

Eis sloshes the wine in her cup, suddenly rocking forward in excitement. "And I get to actually go this year!"

"Yeah, that's right! This will be your first inner court New Year's Eve. We'll have to tell you what you need to prepare. I think this might be my favorite spell."

"I love that we have our own rituals, in addition to the traditional ones," Lore says, smiling big. "Things that are just ours."

Agreement resounds warmly around the room.

These are bonds forged by years of practicing Craft together. These Witches share in each other's magical pursuits, religious explorations, and day-to-day lives. They come from different places and bring different experiences, but together, united by a shared tradition, they've built something that is uniquely theirs.

This is what is means to belong to a coven.

The Witch's Family

One of the most significant differences between traditional and more eclectic styles of Wicca is the role of the coven. Traditional Wicca is coven-based and almost always requires joining some kind of group. You cannot simply read a particular set of books or learn about a tradition on the internet. You must actually seek out a high priestess or high priest in that tradition and ask to be considered for membership in their coven.

No two covens are exactly the same. Even within the same tradition, a great deal of variety may exist. A coven may have a dozen members or only two or three. It may be specifically designed to teach students, or it may be a collective of experienced elders. It may be very highly structured, with a tight calendar of regular meetings, or it may be more casual, meeting only periodically. Depending on the tradition, it may be run by a third degree working couple (a paired high priest and high priestess or a pair of the same gender) or by some council of qualified practitioners. Each tradition has its own protocol, and even within a tradition individual coven leaders usually have the autonomy to make executive decisions, so differences do arise depending on circumstances. In this chapter, we'll look at coven structure and positions within covens. We'll also discuss the functions of covens in detail.

 FROM THE CIRCLE

Coven-based Witchcraft flies in the face of the digital-age trend where personal connections on a frequent basis are few and far between. And in many areas, coven-based Witchcraft offers the chance to connect with hundreds of other Witches for social gatherings of all varieties and traditions. For me, it's one of the few venues where I can have a close and personal connection with people outside of work and family life.

—Thorn Nightwind, priest of the
Horsa and Sacred Pentagraph traditions

Inside a Wiccan Coven

In its earliest stages of development, Wicca was practiced in groups. For many traditions, this continues to be true. Gerald Gardner claimed to have been initiated into a coven, which was the basic unit of organization for Witches. Covens were thought to function within particular territories, serving particular villages and operating as a kind of home base for practitioners within the region. Nearby covens may join together for the celebration of a sabbat or some other event (or to work magic for some larger purpose together, as they supposedly did to protect England from Nazi invasion during World War II, so the famous story of the magical battle for Britain goes), but generally covens were secretive, driven underground by Christian persecution.[5] They existed quietly, passing the secrets of the Craft and the experience of the gods—what we've come to understand as "the Mysteries"—to new generations born to the coven, and bringing in deserving outsiders as they were recognized as one of their own.

Historically, we now understand that many of these early claims are suspect at best. But whatever may have really happened, the coven structure developed and still survives because of its proven value. In short, it works. Group practice makes for highly effective ritual and magical work. It also enables the consistent passing of traditions and the survival and protection of oral lore, which often goes overlooked in more eclectic (and especially solitary) kinds of Wicca. Just like classrooms, covens are often the best learning spaces for new practitioners, who benefit from mentorship, peer feedback, and group discussion. A Witch in a coven always has someone to ask for advice or input. He also benefits from the emotional support that any strong social community may provide to its members.

So how exactly does a Wiccan coven work? And is it different from other kinds of Witchcraft groups? What separates a coven from a study group or open circle?

In its simplest form, a coven is a group of Witches that practices their Craft together. Traditional Wiccan covens are united by a shared praxis. Members share foundational techniques and experiences, which are acquired through a shared training process. Often, there are fundamental religious beliefs and worldviews that are also shared, though these may be assumed upon entrance or otherwise not emphasized formally. Remember, traditional Wicca tends to stress practice over belief. This is

---

5. For more, consult Dion Fortune's *The Magical Battle for Britain,* edited by Gareth Knight (1993). A fictionalized account also exists in Katherine Kurtz's *Lammas Night* (1983).

confusing, especially if you come from a religious background that is grounded in a shared belief system, so allow me to describe an example:

My working partner, Lukaos, and I have been practicing Wicca in the same coven for several years. We work the rites together, train initiates and students together, and share a deep love for our tradition. Our coven, Foxfire, is the product of our partnership. However, our experiences of the gods are sometimes very different. My partner tends to envision the gods in more abstract terms, with a lot of care taken toward his research into various schools of theology. He's well educated in other ways of thinking and tends toward skepticism. He can be somewhat uncomfortable with paradox. It's often useful for him to think about gods in archetypal terms, and he describes himself as a bit of an agnostic. All of this is perfectly acceptable within the context of our tradition, and many other Wiccans feel similar. In contrast, I'm a little more visceral. I don't usually like to think about the gods in those kinds of reasonable, more objective ways, and conversations about theology often bore me. I can't always give you clear explanations for why I believe the things I do (which makes me mostly worthless in debates). I tend to think about gods as discrete entities with human characteristics, and I identify comfortably as a polytheist. I believe that our gods are unique to our tradition and have their own agendas, apart from other gods.

Despite these differences, my partner and I work happily and effectively together, performing the same rites according to the same tradition. We have different beliefs about the nature of the gods—we relate to them differently, we conceive of them differently—but we're both Gardnerians, even trained together in the same coven. Our students have an even greater variety of beliefs about gods. One identifies as an animist; gods become gods insofar as people pour energy and belief into them, and everything has a spirit to it that might be divine. Another came to us as an atheist. For her, gods are psychological constructs that people employ toward practical ends. They impact our lives because we use them to inform our experience of the world. It doesn't matter whether or not they're "real" in any kind of objective way. Any or all of these ideas—plus many more—may exist in a single coven. That the members of Foxfire differ is not an issue, because our individual beliefs are not ultimately what define traditional Wicca. It's our shared practice of the rites that is important. *That* is what makes us Wiccan.

Our coven allows us to mutually create a shared space in which we can perform the rites that are central to our tradition, while also exploring our differences, experimenting with new magical techniques, and perfecting established ones. There's a lot of room for creativity and growth in many directions.

As you can probably imagine, this shared experience leads to a profound level of intimacy. Coven members often become quite close. It is difficult to consistently practice Wicca with a group and not open up to each other over time. You'll share magical experiences—and particularly experiences with the divine—that will set you all apart from the mundane order of your lives. Because of this, there will be some conversations that you can only have with your covenmates. Other people—even other Wiccans outside of your coven—will not be able to relate or understand. This is the nature of the Mysteries, and this shared experience of those Mysteries will create a bond between the members of the coven. Even if you don't socialize outside of circle, even if you're very different kinds of people, you will still share this intimate connection.

Over time, the coven develops its own unique egregore—a group mind. This occurs when coven members fall into a kind of magical rhythm with each other. Just like how best friends and close family members develop the ability to communicate nonverbally and read each other's emotions and thoughts through the tiniest gestures, so covenmates learn to respond to each other magically. Exactly what that entails differs from group to group, but if you can imagine your own experience "reading" and responding to a close friend emotionally, you'll begin to understand how a coven egregore is formed.

Every time someone new is brought into the group (or someone leaves), the egregore shifts. This is why coven leaders take such great care in evaluating and admitting new members. Even if a seeker is well suited to the tradition as a whole, he may not be a good match for the individual coven. This is not to be taken as an insult. Just as we make good friends with some people and not others, so too do we bond with some people magically more naturally than others. This is not by itself a judgment of any person's inherent value.

The bond created between covenmates is a psychic, magical one. It may also be a social or romantic one, but these are rarely the point (though neither is uncommon). Because these are deep psychic bonds, they are often permanent and far-reaching. Even if a covenmate leaves —either temporarily or permanently—their presence may still be felt in circle. Absence becomes palpable. It is never an easy decision to leave, however necessary (and amicable) leaving is.

It is this level of closeness that distinguishes a traditional Wiccan coven from a study group, an open circle, or some other kinds of Pagan groups. Study groups and open circles are necessarily more casual, as typically the requirements to participate are much lower. An environment in which anyone can attend at will with minimal investment rarely, if ever, creates the sort of space that fosters intense magical intimacy. And that's okay! These other kinds of groups serve different but much-needed purposes. It's still beneficial for seekers to participate in these more casual social or educational groups because they have the opportunity to meet others from a variety of magical and religious backgrounds and explore the practice of Witchcraft without the weighty commitment of joining a coven. Many covens even run their own separate study groups, which are more inclusive. A coven may also host open events for a wider community, which foster goodwill, serve the needs of local Pagans, and allow the coven to screen potential members.

But while these more casual groups are sometimes *called* covens in eclectic communities, it's important for seekers to understand that the term has different connotations for most traditional Wiccans. For us, a coven is much more than a reading club, or a group of friends that sometimes meets to mark a sabbat or a full moon. These are good, useful things in their own right, but a coven is an intimate group that enjoys the bond of a shared magical praxis. Membership is exclusive and granted cautiously, usually only after a candidate has been extensively evaluated. Leaders have to make sure that a seeker is both sincerely interested in the specific tradition, and also compatible with the members of that individual coven.

Even amongst traditional covens, there is variety in purpose. Some are designed specifically to accommodate newcomers to the tradition, and these are often called "teaching covens." Teaching covens are normally made up of relatively new initiates and their mentors—maybe a working pair of third degrees, a second degree preparing for elevation, or some combination of elders. In any case, the purpose of a teaching coven is to bring in new members, pass the tradition, and prepare those new members for deeper work.

Other covens are made up entirely (or primarily) of established, seasoned practitioners. These may individually run separate teaching covens, coming together as a body of elders to perform and explore materials and techniques only suitable for the experienced. They could also be Witches who have decided to retire from teaching Craft students or who decided not to become teachers at all. There is something to be said for working only with other initiates of the same rank or skill level, and so some covens restrict their membership in this way.

Most covens are some combination of the above. Rather than talking about types of traditional covens, it may be more useful to think of covens as cycling through stages. Maybe one year a number of new students are initiated. They learn over time and earn their elevations or subsequent initiations, until everyone is a third degree or otherwise a high priest or high priestess in their own right. Some may hive to form their own covens, but others will stay and share the more advanced rites amongst themselves. Eventually, new students may be brought in and the cycle will repeat. So when approaching a coven as a seeker, it may be more accurate to ask if it is accepting new students at this time, rather than to ask if it is a teaching coven.

 FROM THE CIRCLE

Solitary or coven? It's not really either/or. In my very humble opinion, a good covener is also a good solitary. Just because you're in a coven doesn't mean that you stop doing any work or practicing magic on your own. Coven work should help to fuel your solitary work and vice versa. If joining a coven is right for you, don't let that stop your personal work.

—*Phoenix LeFae, Wiccan priestess and Reclaiming Witch*

Roles in the Coven

Aside from a greater sense of intimacy, traditional covens are different from other kinds of Pagan and Wiccan groups in that they tend to be organized according to specific roles. These roles are usually hierarchical, assigned according to individual experience or through passed down authority (and we'll discuss the role of hierarchy in traditional Wicca in a later chapter). Sometimes, these roles are partially determined by gender, though this may vary from coven to coven, especially as new generations of Witches explore nonbinary models. You'll find, too, that some of these roles overlap or exist in some covens and not others:

Initiates: Initiates are those individuals who have been formally, ritually accepted as full members of a tradition. They are no longer seekers or trial members but recognized participants in the coven. Depending on the tradition, initiates are usually ranked, often according to a degree system. In many Wiccan traditions, this is the point at which someone officially earns the title "Witch" and also becomes a priestess or priest. Barring extreme circumstances (which vary across traditions), once one is an initiate, one is *always* an initiate, regardless of subsequent positions bestowed or even the decision to leave the tradition.

First Degree: This is the first level of initiation. First degrees are usually the newest, least experienced initiates, though in some traditions the decision to keep an initiate at first degree may have more to do with nuances in degree obligations. In some covens, for example, second degree initiates are expected to teach their own students. A first degree may choose to stay at first because she does not aspire to teach or to lead a coven, or she may simply be unable to at the time. Sometimes, an initiate's personal life requires additional time spent at first degree, in which case he may be surpassed by more freshly initiated peers, even though he is the more experienced.

Second Degree: In some traditions, second degree Witches earn the right to the title of high priest or high priestess. They take on additional responsibilities in the coven and have access to additional magical knowledge and more advanced techniques. They may be allowed to take on their own students, even running their own outer courts. In some traditions, they are allowed to initiate others into the Craft. In other traditions, this is still only the beginning. First degree may serve as a sort of trial phase, with much of the real work saved for second.

Third Degree: A third degree initiate is a high priestess or high priest of their tradition and has demonstrated mastery within that tradition. A third degree has earned total autonomy and may leave to start her own coven through a process called hiving. Some restrictions may apply, according to the specific tradition, as there is still an obligation to the legacy of the mother coven. Not all third degrees will hive, but they possess the power should they choose to do so. In some traditions, third degree women are entitled to the honorific "Lady." Less frequently, men may take on the title of "Lord," though many traditions eschew this entirely (and referring to yourself as Lord so-and-so is a sure way to give yourself away as a fraud). In either case, such titles are usually reserved for circle, and are not bandied about in public spaces for the sake of ego. Many covens choose not to use such titles at all, viewing them as pretentious and unnecessary.

High Priestess: The high priestess is the female leader of the coven. In many traditions, she is the supreme leader, and this is the highest rank that may be achieved. Often, she is the founder of the coven. Even if there are other third degree priestesses (or second degree priestesses), usually only one serves as the high priestess. In the circle, she is the representative of the goddess. In many traditions, a coven sword symbolizes her power. Final decisions may rest with her, as well as the responsibility of training students. When you approach a coven to inquire about training, more often than not it is her you must persuade.

High Priest: The role of the high priest depends heavily on the tradition. There are covens in which the high priest functions much like the high priestess, described above. If he is the founder and leader, then he will bear the responsibilities of vetting and training students, organizing coven meetings, and so on. In a coven with both a high priestess and a high priest, all of these duties may be shared equally. But in many Wiccan traditions, the high priestess still holds supremacy. The high priest is her consort and support, her helper and guardian. He is the coven's high priest because she has granted him that power in *her* coven. He will help train students, but final decisions rest with the high priestess.

The relationship between a high priestess and high priest is a complex one. In some cases (and this was the ideal in Wicca's early days), they're a married couple or otherwise romantically committed to each other. In other cases, it's more like a sibling relationship, especially if both were trained in the same parent coven and hived together. No matter the specifics, the high priest and high priestess are a team. Each working pair will be different, so these positions may be a bit more fluid than the descriptions I've provided.

Queen: Not all Wiccan traditions have queens. Usually, she is a high priestess whose own initiates have gone on to form their own covens and have initiates of their own. In this sense, she's sort of like a Witch grandmother. In some cases, she must have a certain number of covens descended from her before she is considered a queen (usually three). In others, she must be ritually made a queen in a coronation ritual. She may wear a garter fastened with a buckle for each coven her own initiates found. How much she participates in these covens will vary. She may continue to train students and run her own coven, or she may "retire" from teaching and continue to provide advice and wisdom as an elder.

Magus: As you may have guessed, the magus is the male equivalent of the queen. The magus may have all the responsibilities of a queen in his own right, depending on the tradition, or he may be the consort of a queen. As with queens, magi do not exist in all (or even most) Wiccan traditions. Very, very rarely will you hear a man referred to as a Witch king (and, often, only in reference to Alex Sanders and only as a curious piece of history).

Elder: Elders are those coven members who have the most experience within the group. Usually, these are the third degrees, whether they are serving as high priests and high priestesses or queens and magi. Elder is a relative term, though. A second degree is elder to a first degree, but not to a third, for example. Within the entirety of a tradition, elders are those who have long operated covens and trained students and also those who have made significant contributions in other ways. What's important to understand is that being an elder isn't inherently tied to age. People may come to the Craft at any point in their lives, so physical age is not a fair judge of a Witch's experience. A high priestess in her thirties is still elder to her fifty-year-old first degree. One does not become a queen simply by virtue of aging. Elderhood is about experience in the Craft, not the age of your body.

Elders have a lot of responsibility in the coven, no matter their other roles, because they are always expected to serve as models and guides to newer members of the tradition. Sometimes, they may function directly as mentors to new initiates or they may be asked to run the coven's outer court, a student study group, or other coven-sanctioned learning community.

Maiden or Handmaiden: The maiden of the coven is the female who directly assists the high priestess in circle. Often, she is in training to become high priestess in her own right. She may sometimes serve as high priestess, or give direction and instruction in the high priestess's absence.

Summoner: The summoner is usually a male, and it is his responsibility to organize the coven for ritual, providing practical direction, especially for newcomers. The idea behind the name was that he would "summon" Witches to the sabbat once the coven leaders had finalized their intentions. In some situations, he would also stand outside the circle, armed and guarding the coven against intruders, whether physical or magical. I have seen this use of a summoner at open rituals and at outdoor events on public land, but it's less common for smaller groups and groups that meet on private property. I've also seen the position of summoner filled by a woman (and have filled it myself!). It's also possible to see a summoner serving as assistant to the high priest, as the maiden is to the high priestess.

The roles of maiden and summoner are common in some traditions and totally absent from others. Sometimes, they are not permanent positions, but individual coven members may rotate these duties. Very small covens may have no need for them at all.

The remaining three coven roles have a greater variety in usage across Wiccan traditions and in individual covens. It's not uncommon for these terms to be used interchangeably. According to mundane definitions, their meanings are very similar:

Neophyte: A neophyte is someone in the process of becoming something. The term is usually used to refer to someone preparing for initiation. In some traditions, like Blue Star Wicca, neophyte is a ritually acknowledged stage in a series of rites of passage. These are individuals who have formally asked for initiation, and whom the coven leaders have decided are ready to begin formally working toward it.

Dedicant: Usually, a dedicant is an acknowledged student of a coven. Often, this position is marked with a formal dedication ritual. In most cases, she has taken no oaths and is not formally a member of the coven. This is a discovery period, when a seeker may learn about a tradition firsthand, before bearing the weight of responsibility that comes with initiation.

Student: Sometimes, this is a formal position, where a student is someone (like a neophyte) who is formally working toward initiation. A student may be someone who's been formally accepted into an outer court. Really, we never stop being students. Even a high priestess may continue to defer to her *own* high priestess years after the fact.

FROM THE CIRCLE

One of my favorite things about being in a coven is not just having a community, but having a *family*. This feels especially important to me because I come from a small family (I'm an only child) and we aren't very close. I revel in family dinner together before circle, exchanging gifts at the winter solstice, or just knowing that I have Craft siblings that I could call on if

I ever needed anything. I also enjoy meeting extended family (my high priestess's coven siblings are like aunts and uncles, and my queen is like a grandmother) and hearing old stories about my upline.

—*Corvus, Wiccan initiate*

Outer Courts

Due to the publishing boom and the media attention that Gerald Gardner, Alex and Maxine Sanders, and others attracted, the public interest in Wicca soon surpassed the number of covens that had space for seekers. Qualified people might be turned away simply because a working high priestess or high priest could only reasonably take on so many students at once. Further, some seekers were interested in practicing the Craft or worshipping the old gods but didn't necessarily feel called to become priests or priestesses, devoting themselves to a larger community or running covens of their own. It became necessary to devise a strategy for handling newcomers—one that would allow a coven to accommodate larger numbers, more time to screen potential initiates, and a way to train those who belonged in the religion without requiring that they commit such a large part of their lives to it.

Outer courts provided a solution. Developed primarily in the eighties by author and Gardnerian high priest Ed Fitch, a training system called the Pagan Way arose to prepare seekers for life in a coven. Members of a coven usually oversaw Pagan Way groups. They had their own rituals, activities for beginning magical practice, and even their own deities. Seekers spent time in the coven's Pagan Way group (or sometimes just "Pagan" group) and then went on to become initiates. Others, however, chose to stay in the Pagan Way, and many of these groups came to be independent, with their own leadership, their own developing traditions, and no desire to enter the Witch priesthood formally. Pagan Way materials were published in assorted popularly available books—notably Ed Fitch's *Magical Rites from the Crystal Well* (1984) and *A Grimoire of Shadows* (1996)—and were quickly absorbed into a wider Pagan movement, particularly in the United States. Many of the wider Pagan community's most well-loved rituals, techniques, chants, and beliefs arose from expansion and development of the Pagan Way. One of the reasons why "generic Paganism" (as though that could ever fairly be an objective thing) looks so much like Wicca is because of the spread of the Pagan Way.

These Pagan Way groups were also called outer courts, with the initiates making up an inner court, in contrast. Other groups use different terms (including grove, training circle, and others), but the basic premise is the same: a ritual group for would-be Witches, designed to prepare seekers for future participation in a formal coven. Sometimes, there is a set curriculum and a minimum timeframe during which students must participate and complete a set assortment of tasks. Often, however, the training process is individualized. Some outer court groups are very informal, functioning more like book clubs or discussion groups. Usually, there is some ritual component, but every group is different.

Running an outer court alongside a coven (or inner court) is a huge job. Coven leaders may delegate the task to experienced second or even first degrees. Sometimes, outer court students will be kept completely separate from initiates. Other times inner and outer courts are combined, with shared rituals being appropriate for noninitiates. Outer court members may have mentors in the coven and often meet with coven leaders individually for discussion and individualized training.

In seeking to join a traditional coven and become a Wiccan priestess or priest, the first step is often asking to join a coven's outer court. This process allows the high priestess and high priest to assess seekers over time for sincerity and compatibility. It also allows the seeker to make an informed decision before committing to either a coven or a whole tradition. The specifics of outer court participation—what's included in training and how long one can expect to remain in outer court—can vary considerably from coven to coven. Some covens may not employ an outer court model at all, choosing to evaluate potential initiates in other ways before committing to them. You may be asked to attend social events with coven members or to otherwise spend time with the leaders more casually to gauge your fit with the group.

We will discuss the finer points of joining and succeeding in an outer court (or other kind of training group) in part 3, as well as what to expect!

CHAPTER 3

INITIATION

Perhaps the most well-known and discussed (not to mention controversial) characteristic of traditional Wicca is its emphasis on initiation. Traditional Wicca is a priesthood that requires formal admission. You can't just read a few books and declare yourself a member. You must seek out a traditional coven or teacher and be initiated. But what exactly does that mean? What does initiation entail? Does it really make you different from other kinds of Wiccans? Can you initiate yourself? Is there a difference between initiation and dedication? Why is this such a hot-button issue in Wiccan communities?

What Is Initiation?

For the clearest understanding of what initiation is and how it works, it's useful to consider the term as it applies more broadly, particularly in other cultural and religious contexts. Initiation isn't a concept that's unique to Wicca, after all! Let's take a look at a technical, academic standpoint to get us started.

Contemporary understandings of initiation are closely tied to the work of three very important scholars of the twentieth century: Arnold van Gennep, Victor Turner, and Joseph Campbell. Arnold van Gennep (1873–1957) was a German-born, French-educated anthropologist and ethnographer, well known for his book *Les rites de passage* (1909). Based on his own ethnographic work (which means that he actually spent time with the people he was studying) and literary study of (primarily European) folklore, he argued that rites of passage have three fundamental stages: separation, transition, and incorporation.

Here's an example of what he's talking about:

For the Xhosa, a South African tribal group (with the distinction, by the way, of having had Nelson Mandela as a member), boys, usually in their late teens and early twenties, become men by undergoing circumcision. When they are deemed ready, they're removed from their homes and families to live together in small, specially constructed houses outside the village. Their heads are shorn, their bodies are painted, and they participate in a number of rituals, culminating in circumcision. Afterwards, they must stay outside of their village for a period of several months. They observe special dietary restrictions, perform additional rituals, and wear special clothes. When this period is over, the boys wash the paint from their bodies, burn their ritually prepared houses, and return home, where they are reincorporated into daily life, now as men.[6]

This example embodies the three stages of a rite of passage as described by van Gennep really clearly. The boys are separated from their communities, undergo a transformation, and are then welcomed back into society, their change in station publically acknowledged in the village.

Another anthropologist named Victor Turner (1920–1983) later elaborated on this process in his own work on initiation and its application within a religious framework. Turner described van Gennep's three-stage process in terms of "liminality," which is the state of being in between two points. Initiation—what van Gennep might call "transformation"—represents the period of transition from one way of being to another, especially within a particular community. Joseph Camp-

6. Heather Montgomery, "A Comparative Perspective," in *Understanding Youth: Perspectives, Identities & Practices*, ed. Mary Jane Kehily (London: Sage Publishing, 2007), 62–66.

bell (1904–1987), our third scholar, was heavily influenced by Victor Turner when he was working on his own ideas about the hero's journey. The hero's journey is a narrative formula that Campbell initially detailed in his work *The Hero with a Thousand Faces* (1949). Campbell posited that this archetypal story—which he called a "monomyth"—could be found throughout the world, uniting humanity through shared experience. Campbell incorporated Turner and van Gennep more broadly in his understanding of folklore. Thanks to these three thinkers, today's anthropologists, religious studies scholars, and folklorists still consider initiation with an understanding that it is tied to both transformation and community.

Rites of passage help us collectively mark and process life changes. These are changes that we may go through anyway—like puberty, childbirth, or death—but they take on further meaning when we acknowledge them communally, through ritual. An initiation is distinct from other rites of passage because it involves the movement from one state of being to another, with a transitional (Turner would say "liminal") stage in between. Additionally—according to the scholarly definition we've examined—that process is social. What ultimately changes is the individual's place *in the community.*

In traditional Wicca, initiation marks the seeker's transformation from outsider to insider. No longer a student in an outer court, they become a full-fledged priestess or priest, accepted as a Witch and full member of the coven. Further, they become a member of the tradition as a whole, with whatever rights and responsibilities that may entail.

The exact ritual of initiation may vary from tradition to tradition. Most covens are very secretive about this process. Partially, this secrecy is in place to lend power to the rite itself. Secrets *feel* powerful and can make the experience that much more profound. More simply, secrecy protects a coven's privacy. There's no reason for outsiders to know details because there is no context for the experience outside of the tradition itself. Finally, this secrecy helps to deepen the shared experience of members in the tradition. Knowing that they've all joined via the same rite creates a profound bond that unites members of a community. But whatever the specifics of the ritual or events leading up to the ritual, a Wiccan initiation is something that Arnold van Gennep, Victor Turner, and Joseph Campbell would all recognize.

Given that an initiation is a ritual recognition of a person's change in social status, it's easy to say that initiates are necessarily different from noninitiates (which includes other kinds of Wiccans). Initiation confers upon an individual new responsibility within the group, as well as certain privileges. It's a social contract—an agreement in a community. And it's the social nature of this agreement that brings us to another significant point: rites of passage (like initiations) do not necessarily transfer across group lines. An initiation into a tradition (or coven) does not automatically confer initiation into another.

Think back to van Gennep and the Xhosa. That was just one case of a rite of passage from boyhood to manhood. In other groups, the process looks very different. Jewish boys, as another example, become men in the eyes of their community by going through the ritual of Bar Mitzvah. Other groups have their own markers of manhood, only some of which may be celebrated ritually (having sex for the first time, making a first kill during a hunt, going to war, etc.). What's important to understand is that the concept of "manhood" does not manifest in the same way in every case. It would be unreasonable to expect members of one group to unquestioningly accept the "men" of another given that the context is different. Similarly, a priest of one tradition of Wicca is not automatically a priest of another tradition. An initiation into my coven doesn't grant you membership in another coven. Likewise, I don't extend invitations and hand out secrets to other Witches just because they've been initiated into someone else's coven. There are absolutely cases in which initiations *are* acknowledged across group and tradition lines, but this should not be *assumed.*

 FROM THE CIRCLE

Initiation should never be taken on lightly. In our modern Pagan world it sometimes feels like folks collect initiations like college degrees in order to have the title, and that's *so* not the right reason. I'm a Reclaiming Tradition initiate, a Gardnerian Wicca initiate, a Druid initiate, and self-initiated. These traditions and initiations are vastly different, some of them being (almost) on opposite ends of the initiation spectrum. My initiations were all a part of my personal spiritual development, folding in knowledge and faith from different vantage points. Each initiation has been woven into the complex tapestry that is me, and they all came at different points in my life.

—*Phoenix LeFae, Wiccan priestess and Reclaiming Witch*

Self-Initiation

So is it possible to initiate yourself into Wicca?

Since Wicca's early days, this has been a point of contention, especially after so many publications became so readily available. As we've discussed, it didn't take long for seekers to outnumber available space in established covens. Many turned to books (and to each other) for information on practicing without a coven. Many joined Pagan Way groups, outer courts, and other kinds of Witchcraft groups. Collectively, these groups designed their own rites and traditions, leading many to become accomplished Witches without ever receiving initiation into a traditional coven. There were even Wiccan elders who advocated these kinds of strategies in the absence of covens or initiated teachers, Doreen Valiente being one of the most notable.[7] As time went on and more books and (later) online resources became more available, this process of self-teaching became even easier and more widespread.

---

7. Doreen Valiente, *Witchcraft for Tomorrow* (Custer, WA: Phoenix Publishing, 1978), 159–64.

Eclectic styles of Wicca developed into their own traditions, and solitary practice became commonplace. Many claimed to have initiated themselves, and increasingly these Witches demanded the respect and acknowledgment of Wiccans who had been formally trained in traditional covens. Today, self-teaching and solitary practice are the norm, with these kinds of Witches outnumbering those in covens.[8] Few of the most prominent Wiccan writers, teachers, and online personalities are initiates as was understood in the mid-twentieth century.

Reactions to this over the years have been mixed. Some early traditionalists accepted these self-taught practitioners as Wiccans in their own right, and even went on to advocate for this sort of learning. Gardnerian priest Ray Buckland, who was one of the people responsible for bringing traditional Wicca to the United States, famously split from his coven and published a variety of books designed to help solitaries and eclectics build their own traditions. He even founded his own form of Witchcraft: Seax-Wica. Others held to those stringent boundaries, arguing that Wicca is a priesthood that requires specific training, as well as the magical authority that is conferred upon initiation into a coven. All along, others have taken a kind of middle position, observing that, ultimately, Wicca is about devotion to the gods. It is *they* who choose their priests and priestesses. Who could possibly have more authority in matters of belonging and initiation?

Many have made compelling cases for all these perspectives as well as others I haven't even mentioned. A lot of ink has been spilled over this issue. The role of initiation might be the most divisive controversy in Wicca's history. In the 1990s and early 2000s, this argument became downright nasty, with the development of terms like "fluffy bunny," which were flung around the internet to disparage this new

---

8. Helen A. Berger, Evan A. Leach, and Leigh S. Shaffer, *Voices from the Pagan Census: A National Survey of Witches and Neo-Pagans in the United States* (Columbia: University of South Carolina Press, 2003), 114–18.

Wiccan movement.[9] Eclectic Wiccans responded with their own vitriol, and traditionalists developed a reputation for being judgmental, self-righteous, and stuck in the past.

So who's right? Can you just initiate yourself? And if not, then who can initiate you? The gods? A high priestess? What about a single high priest? Someone of the same gender? And why does everyone's answer seem to be different?

I'll go ahead and spoil the ending for you: I'm not going to give you a straight, perfectly satisfying answer to any of these questions. We'll probably be fighting over this issue for generations to come. What I *will* do is explain the mechanics of initiation and lineage within traditional Wicca so that the value that traditionalists place on initiation at least makes sense to you. You may come to different conclusions (and you'll have plenty of company, no matter what position you take), but at least these arguments will be clear.

The crux of initiation—as we've discussed it so far—is that it's social. Whether we're talking about becoming a man or becoming a Wiccan, the whole point is that the individual transitions from one position *in society* to another. Rites of passage, according to the scholars we've considered, are communal events. They have meaning only in social contexts. For a traditional Wiccan, initiation is the acceptance of a new member into the tradition. Depending on the tradition, the initiate may receive special ritual tools, the secret names of deities, or other ritual-magical authority (and ability). But in any case, what she always receives is *membership*. For this reason, from this perspective, there can be no self-initiation. Another must bestow initiation upon you. You cannot simply declare yourself a member of a group whose mark for membership is a ritualized rite of passage.

---

9. One of the most prominent instigators was the anonymous author of the now-defunct website www.whywicanssuck.com. You can still find leftover fragments preserved here: "Why Wiccans Suck," OoCities, accessed January 4, 2018, http://www.oocities.org/whywiccansstillsuck/.

In this sense, becoming a traditional Wiccan initiate is a little like becoming a doctor or becoming a Catholic priest. In the case of the former, I would have to go to medical school, survive a formal residency, and become licensed by a medical board to practice medicine, according to a set standard. Collectively, we've agreed (even tacitly) that this is what qualifies someone to be a doctor, and these are the people who we seek out when we need medical care. If we encounter someone who cannot provide these credentials, we become suspicious. They could write MD after their name all day long, but they're never going to get hired in a hospital. Becoming a doctor is a process defined and enforced by a *group*. Further, it bears particular markers that we learn to look for and recognize: a degree, a license, references, fluency with a particular jargon (medical terms), and, of course, competence. Anyone could declare themselves to be a doctor, but it wouldn't make it true.

Similarly, a Catholic priest becomes a Catholic priest by attending a particular kind of seminary, publically taking a particular set of vows, and undergoing a ritual passing of authority within the Catholic Church. He then goes on to work within the Church, in whatever capacity he is needed, as befits his calling. His priesthood is verifiable within his community and recognized in the same way that doctors are recognizable, according to a different set of earmarks. Someone could declare themselves to be a Catholic priest, but this declaration alone would not make it so.

Being a Wiccan and training in a coven isn't like going to med school or seminary whole cloth, but it is similar in that all three of these positions—doctor, Catholic priest, traditional Wiccan—are acquired through a training process administered by other people. I can't just read a lot of books and call myself a doctor. I can't recite the ritual to become ordained as a Catholic priest in my bedroom and instantly become a Catholic priest. Even if I used the titles and learned the jargon, no one in medical or Catholic communities would support my claim. Likewise, I can't pull a copy of a traditional Wiccan initiation ritual off the internet, perform it, and then expect the local Alexandrian coven to have me over for circle willy-nilly. Not only will they not greet me with open arms, I'll likely become the butt of some jokes, having offended the community by disregarding their accepted protocol.

This position—that initiation is a social act conferring membership into a group—carries an underlying assumption that lends important clarity. We are assuming that initiation necessarily entails the passing of a skill set, particularly one that is unobtainable outside of the group. This makes traditional Wicca somewhat unique when compared to other spiritual traditions; part of being an initiate entails the cultivation of ability.[10] You're not just receiving membership; you're receiving special knowledge. This is in keeping with our analogy about medical school. You don't just magically get the right to be called doctor; you earn it through the demonstration of an elite skill set. This skill set is experiential (we'll talk more about what that means in chapter 6) and complex enough that it requires significant input from teachers and a cohort of peers. Thus, the process of going to medical school is inherently different from only reading medical textbooks. Further, there is an oral component that cannot be replicated by simply reading.

Traditional Wicca is much the same. Initiation isn't just about membership. It's also about access to special knowledge and the ability to demonstrate some kind of proficiency in the more practical tasks that go along with Craft practice (such as organizing a group ritual, performing a particular piece of liturgy, or creating your own spells within the tradition). The specifics of both vary with tradition. Reading books or websites about traditional Wicca is not the equivalent of receiving the oral lore of a coven, or gaining practical experience in a Wiccan

---

10. Which is not to say that every member must possess the *same* skills or the same level of proficiency at any given thing. You will have your own talents and interests!

environment. For that reason, self-initiation isn't usually feasible or ac-knowledged.

There are counterarguments, naturally. Many have been devel-oped at length, especially by other kinds of Wiccans. There's no two-ways about it: if we agree with the argument I've just presented, we necessarily include some people while excluding others. It makes for a Wicca that is *not* inherently open and welcoming. It is available to some and not to others, and sometimes for reasons that are totally be-yond the control of the seeker. What if you are dedicated and sincere, but you simply don't live near enough to a working coven? What if you work the night shift and the local coven only meets when you're unavailable? What if you don't own a car? Or don't have the extra cash to pay for a babysitter?

We'll talk more about these and other practical issues in part 3, but for now, understand this: anytime you're talking about something that has set rules for participation and membership, some people end up being excluded. This always has the potential to hurt feelings and create anger. Many of the counterarguments to the exclusivity of ini-tiation find footing on these grounds. Dedication and sincerity must count for something, surely? While they may be rare, isn't it possible that a very gifted mind could engage with the same medical textbooks and learn to heal? Isn't it possible to perform medicine in an emer-gency and save lives, without the formality of schooling? What about alternative healing? Don't we all learn at least a little bit about health-care just by virtue of surviving in the world? And, further, aren't some doctors just incompetent?

Yes. To all of these.

There are to-the-letter initiates in the world with no sense of com-mitment to either tradition or to the gods. There are Wiccan high priestesses and high priests who seem to have no magical proclivities at all, who may not be Witches by most definitions beyond title. There are self-taught, solitary, eclectic Wiccans who could outdo them—both in passion and ability—at every turn. There are Witches who *should* be brought in—who deserve it—but who simply haven't had fair access or opportunity. And there are Witches who should never have been initiated at all, who bring shame to their covens and do disservice to their traditions. In my experience, initiation cannot be taken as the only indicator of merit or even the primary indicator. It is only a first step.

It's not a perfect system. Many have argued that Craft proficiency can be developed outside of covens and formal initiations, so those who demonstrate this proficiency should be acknowledged as members. This may be reasonable for some traditions and in certain circumstances, but it really depends on what you think initiation is and what it does. If it conveys knowledge, then initiation may become moot if that knowledge can be acquired elsewhere. If it conveys social status within a group, then only the group can bestow it.

And what about the gods? Surely they play some part in all this.

In many traditions, it is at initiation that the Witch meets the gods. In these cases, the identity of the gods is a protected secret. Only members of the tradition know whom they worship.[11] A formal introduction is necessary because that is the nature of those particular gods. Now, as we've already discussed, traditional Wicca tends to be orthopraxic rather than orthodoxic (and we'll dissect these terms at some length in chapter 6). There is no simple, agreed-upon experience of the gods. Some Wiccans believe that the gods act in our lives whether we are initiated into a coven or not. Initiation may reveal a set of secret names or a special body of rituals, but the gods may manifest in other ways to other people. Theoretically, you could have access to them outside of the confines of any one coven's experience of them. Other Wiccans believe that these gods are unique to their tradition and only respond to members of that tradition. In this case, formal introduction through

---

11. In fact, one of the reasons Wiccans today have a reputation for worshipping a "generic" Lord and Lady is because traditional Wiccans used these titles in place of their names. Eclectic Wiccans, having never received these identities, plugged in others.

initiation is essential. The gods do not reveal themselves to outsiders. Another perspective is that the gods are a manifestation of the egregore of the coven. When you're initiated, you become part of this egregore and can access the gods from this unique standpoint.

All this is to say that whether or not you think the gods are ultimately the source of authority where initiation is concerned depends entirely on your beliefs about the nature of the gods! And there is so much variety within Wicca with regard to the nature of the gods that, no matter your position, you'll have plenty of opponents. Many have claimed to be initiated by the gods, but what exactly does this mean? And what should we expect it to mean to other people? Again, we mostly find ourselves in a position where we can assert our belonging all day long, but it would be unreasonable to expect people with different beliefs and experiences to accept us into their groups unchallenged. Do the gods play a role in initiation? Absolutely. But what exactly that role is will depend on the tradition and the individual coven.

You may have had internal transformative experiences that you feel are initiatory—whether or not the gods were involved or whether or not you feel like you've attained mastery of some skill or other—and those are important. They propel your practice forward and represent personal milestones. Regardless of the type of Craft you practice, no one can take those away from you. Traditional Wiccan initiation is transformative but with the added dimension of belonging to a group.

Dedication

As a precursor to initiation—or sometimes instead of it—many employ a ritual of dedication. Where initiation marks acceptance within a particular group and is bestowed by someone else upon the initiate, dedication is a commitment on the part of the individual. Whether it takes place in a formal group setting or is performed by a solitary practitioner, a dedication marks a conscious decision to commit time and energy to a particular deity, to a tradition, or just more generally to the study and practice of Witchcraft. Usually, this dedication is ritualized somehow. You may set aside some time and formally declare your intentions, perhaps directly to the gods, to witnesses in a group, or, at the very least, only to yourself. You may agree to a set course of study, to engage in a particular practice, or to adopt a particular lifestyle, usually for a set period of time. At the end of that time, you may reevaluate, either making different choices or committing to your path more permanently.

Usually, dedication represents an initial step on a new path. Many covens perform dedication rituals for new members of outer courts, or they encourage seekers to write and perform their own privately, before they've been accepted into any particular group. Formal dedication is a way to lend seriousness to practically any new pursuit, in the same way that signing up for a class is often more serious than reading about a subject casually. Usually, you would take some time to research and experiment on your own before dedicating to any religious or magical practice.

Many seekers write their own dedication rituals or find a meaningful way to improvise them in private. Most introductory Wiccan books contain ideas for what these might look like and even include rituals that you may modify for your own purposes. If dedication takes place in a group context, seekers may take on additional rank and responsibility in the group. For many outer courts and groves, this is the point at which the seeker officially becomes a student. Usually, this is a limited period during which both the student and the coven leaders evaluate each other for compatibility. The student may decide that either the tradition or the individual coven isn't a good fit after all, and then he would be free to leave and seek elsewhere with no harm done. Likewise, the coven may decide that the student is a poor fit or otherwise unsuited for initiation.

Dedication is a serious step, but in many ways it's a type of trial period. It's not uncommon for seekers to move in other directions over the course of dedication. For this reason, dedication is usually nonbinding. In a coven setting, a ritual dedication almost never includes the passing of lineage, magical power, secrets, or core materials. In this way, dedication is fundamentally distinct from initiation. Initiation is a binding process. Even if an initiate someday leaves the tradition—and this absolutely happens—that rite of passage isn't undone. You can't unknow an experience any more than you can revert to childhood after becoming an adult. An effective initiatory experience causes fundamental change. You never completely return to your prior state, even if your path eventually leads elsewhere.

A powerful dedication may have a similar effect, but it does not carry the weight of a tradition. In some ways, dedication is a more personal experience. It can lead to profound personal change, though it is necessarily distinct from initiation.

Initiation in Wicca is a complex—and controversial—issue. There aren't any clear answers that apply to every tradition and every coven. Generally, we seem to agree that initiation is important. It's one of the earmarks of traditional Wicca, distinguishing it from other types. It's a rite of passage marking a person as a member of a group. The specifics of that rite will vary from tradition to tradition, but that centrality of the group is the reason why self-initiation is rarely acknowledged in traditional communities. You can't give yourself access to a closed community any more than you can walk uninvited into a stranger's house and demand to be part of the family. Membership must be earned. Someone who is already inside the house must invite you in, and this is an act of profound trust. Every coven has its own standards, and every tradition has its own process.

Where initiation isn't available or isn't appropriate, a dedication ritual may be the best course of action. The decision to dedicate can be a very profound one, and it often takes place privately, in the seeker's own time. It's not the same as initiation, but it can have similar emotional effects. Both types of ritual represent significant rites of passage and mark forward progress in the Craft.

 FROM THE CIRCLE

I performed a personal dedication in the woods behind my house about two months after I started *devouring* books on Witchcraft and Paganism. There was a point at which I decided this was a real thing for me, that I needed to announce to myself and the world in a formal way that I was committed to following this path, wherever it might take me. I wasn't really talking about this with my husband at that point (I was very shy and a little embarrassed about it, actually), so I waited until my family was out of town for a few days. I took a small plate of cookies and a double shot of cinnamon whiskey into the woods. I spent a while grounding and centering. That alone still felt monumentally dedicating. I'd written out words I was going to speak, but ended up speaking extemporaneously, and I was bawling by the end, but just so happy, so excited. People say it feels like coming home … It really did. I left the cookies and whiskey in the woods for the gods and went back home and had more myself. It was a great day and I really did feel transformed.

—*Wren, first degree priestess*

CHAPTER 4

LINEAGE

Initiation into a traditional Wiccan coven confers lineage onto the new initiate. Most simply, lineage is a way of articulating a connection within a group, especially a family. Children trace their lineage through their parents, usually in the form of a surname. When we follow that line through history we find grandparents, great grandparents, and on and on. We may also find aunts and uncles, cousins, and siblings, all with the same connection. Even if a family doesn't share a single surname (few do, these days), they share connections through blood, marriage, and adoption. We use these connections in legal situations, to pass property, for example, or to determine who should be responsible for children in the event that a parent dies. We also use them socially, to build relationships and further reputations. If a stranger comes to your door, you're usually more likely to invite them in if they can demonstrate that they're actually related to you somehow. Similarly, we use our family connections (if we can) to find jobs, to find new places to live when we move, and to otherwise expand our social networks. Some families carry substantial legacies, having made significant historical contributions, gained notoriety through public scandal, or simply because they've accrued massive amounts of wealth. Consider, for example, what it would mean to be born a Windsor in England or a Kennedy in the United States. How might this be different from being born a Kardashian? A Genovese? A Rockefeller?

Lineage carries meaning beyond any individual. A lineage is a network, and having a particular lineage carries certain ramifications, whatever that lineage may be.

Traditional Wiccans possess initiatory lineage. Just like children trace their parental lineage through their mother and father to grandparents and then to great grandparents, a traditional Wiccan traces her lineage to her initiator and then to their initiator, and so on. This lineage is traced to the founder of the tradition, and sometimes beyond (depending on which version of history you prefer). A Gardnerian Wiccan, for example, belongs to a lineage that can be traced, step-by-step, to Gerald Gardner and one of his high priestesses. An Alexandrian Wiccan possesses a lineage that can be traced to Alex Sanders. Other traditions stem from their own founders, though they may not be named after them (incidentally, Alexandrian Wicca is actually named for the ancient Library of Alexandria in Egypt, not Sanders himself). Sometimes one Witch may be able to trace his lineage to more than one founder because—somewhere along the line—someone (either himself or maybe one of his initiators) was initiated into more than one tradition and passed both. This individual is said to have dual lineage. Even in these cases, usually one lineage takes precedence over the other, for various reasons, according to the individual Witch.

According to definitions we've discussed, initiation marks the passage from one state to another. This does not, in and of itself, confer lineage. Becoming a man, joining a fraternity, or graduating from a university may all represent types of initiation rituals, but they don't usually carry the weight of a familial line. Becoming a traditional Wiccan entails both initiation and lineage. When a Wiccan speaks of initiation, he means the ritual act of becoming a Witch. When he speaks of lineage, he means the particular family line that conferred that initiation. In traditional Wicca, initiation and lineage are closely linked—one comes with the other—but they remain distinct things that warrant individual consideration for seekers.

There is an important paradox present in traditional Wicca, which you may have already discerned: development in the Craft is a solitary pursuit, and yet it takes place in a social setting. Your spiritual progress and your relationship with the gods and the seasonal cycles are personal, yet that progress is measured in the context of a coven. In addition to your individual experiences, you'll also have group experiences and a shared body of knowledge from which to start. Part of this group experience is tied to your lineage. Within your tradition—which may be quite large, including so many people that you could never meet all of them—you have your more immediate family. These people will impact you, coloring and defining your personal experiences within the wider tradition. This is true of most any social experience: the quality of the people you spend time with necessarily impacts the thing itself. In traditional Wicca, lineage is one of the things we use to consider quality, though this is not always overt.

 FROM THE CIRCLE

In a coven, there is a connection that is so much greater than anything I could have ever fathomed having. We've made a commitment to work and grow in the same place, at the same time, and I can draw on that magical and emotional connection whenever I need to. For me, it is beyond value or measure. To those who follow this path—who chose to allow themselves to be chosen by the gods—there is no other place to be.

—*Rayn, Gardnerian high priestess*

Lineage and Legitimacy

As we've already discussed, traditional Wicca is distinct from other kinds of Wicca in that traditions share a core body of rites and lore that is passed from experienced members to new members. Each generation of practitioners inherits this collection of shared knowledge, with its key materials fundamentally unchanged. This is what makes the tradition a tradition, instead of just a collection of different covens. The integrity of this inheritance is a primary function of lineage.

Let's think back for a moment to an analogy from the last chapter. In our discussion of initiation, I likened becoming a traditional Wiccan to training as a doctor. Doctors go to special schools, study, practice, and are ultimately certified by an external body that grants them authority. If we continue with this analogy, lineage represents the medical student's professors, advisors, and perhaps the particular school that she chooses to attend. Lineage is a question of who does the training and ultimately takes responsibility for the education of the student. There are many doctors in the world, but each may have very different teachers. The quality of the new doctor is largely dependent on the quality of those teachers. Further, some teachers will have had longer careers, better track records, better reputations, or just greater rapport with students. It's neither a perfect system nor a perfect analogy—lackluster medical schools turn out excellent doctors, and brilliant professors don't guarantee competent students—but, generally, we tend to believe that we can reasonably expect certain levels of quality from our medical professionals based on where they were trained. Similarly, we find that knowing another Wiccan's lineage can tell us something about what he knows and how he practices his Craft.

It is for this reason that lineage often becomes such a serious and sensitive subject in traditional Wiccan communities. If we think of lineage as a chain, then it stands to reason that a weakness in one link impacts the integrity of the whole. When someone asks, "What is your coven's lineage?" what they are often really asking is, "Did you come from someone I can trust and respect?" This is, of course, another way of asking, "Are you *really* one of us?" And *that* is an intimate, touchy question indeed.

So what constitutes a weak link in the chain? What might call someone's legitimacy into question, and who gets to decide?

As you might have guessed, the answer to that question is going to vary widely depending on whom you ask (and perhaps on what day you ask them). Some traditions, for example, place an emphasis on a particular initiation ritual and accompanying protocol. If that ritual isn't carried out according to a particular standard, the validity of the initiate may be called into question, especially by those outside the immediate coven or line. It may also be a question of witnesses to subsequently vouch for that initiate. If no one can verify that a ritual took place, the initiate's validity may, again, be called into question. Further—and maybe most significantly—there are questions in many traditions about what constitutes the "core" that must be passed. What elements of a tradition must be left unchanged in order for that tradition to be recognizable? Is there a limit to what can be changed—added or removed—before it becomes something else entirely? Most traditional Wiccans would say yes, of course, but we don't all agree on where that limit is. The result is that, over time, an individual strand within a wider tradition (what we call a "line") may alter the core to such an extent that other strands no longer consider those individuals to be practicing the tradition.

Imagine this:

High priestess Glinda decides that she has no use for flying monkeys in her practice of Witchcraft. Her tradition has always had flying monkeys—every initiate gets one of their own when they're initiated—but Glinda finds the whole thing unnecessary. Maybe she just thinks they're smelly and offensive. Or maybe she believes she's found a historical precedent for *not* having flying monkeys. Maybe she thinks "flying monkeys" was really a misunderstanding on the part of early practitioners, and everyone is really supposed to have flying cats. Whatever the reason, she does away with the monkeys.

If I were in Glinda's original initiating coven (me and my monkey), am I necessarily going to think Glinda is practicing the same tradition? What if I'm part of another flying monkey coven, twenty years down the line, and I meet someone at a festival who tells me we're part of the same tradition and then pulls out a flying cat? What might I think? What conclusion could I reasonably draw?

If this sounds stupid to you, just replace "flying monkey" with "transubstantiation" or some similarly significant point of religious controversy. Religious groups have been doing this sort of thing for a long time. Wiccans are no exception. We draw lines, erect boundaries, and set standards. Whether or not those lines and standards are reasonable depends on who you are and what the context is (and, more often than not, whether or not you yourself are going to be excluded). What looks like a weak link in a person's lineage may be a strength to someone else.

What seekers need to understand is that these boundaries exist.

In many larger Witchcraft traditions, numerous lineages may exist within a number of different lines. These lines are defined over time by characteristics that make them unique. Over generations of initiates, lines come to have distinct customs and defining personalities. Depending on how much information is readily available, a seeker may learn about the various lines within a tradition and decide to approach one versus another for a variety of reasons. Within my own tradition, for example, there are many lines. In Gardnerian communities, you'll hear talk of CalGards, Proteans, the Old Kentucky line, the Long Island line, Whitecroft, Silver Circle, the Florida line, and others. Often, the difference between these lies in one charismatic high priestess or high priest, putting their own signature on some aspect of the tradition (even unintentionally) and then propagating it through generations of initiates who may not even realize that they've become markedly distinct from those outside their own Craft family. The validity of one line may be refuted by another, though both vehemently claim ownership of the Gardnerian label.

These differences in practice may be relatively small, such as a slight difference in altar arrangement or in the use of a particular tool. They may also be quite substantial, as in a different hierarchical structure or a different interpretation of a core rite. Individual lines may acquire particular reputations (for being "hard-line" or "elaborate" or "loosey-goosey" or "liberal" or some such, depending on who's doing the describing), which may in turn reflect on its initiates, for good or ill. How much change is too much and what changes are big or small will depend on individual perspective.

Seekers can begin to learn about Wiccan traditions and the variations within them in a variety of ways. Many begin with the more well-known traditions and then discover others over time. Before picking up this book, you may have heard of Gardnerian and Alexandrian Wicca, but consider others: the Georgian tradition, Central Valley Wicca, the Mohsian tradition, Blue Star Wicca, Keepers of the Ancient Mysteries, the Minoan Brotherhood, the Algard tradition, and the American Welsh tradition. Some of the more established traditions have texts available detailing general histories, schisms, and changes introduced by prominent leaders (and you can find some of these in this book's further reading section). In the age of the internet, it's become relatively easy to find online communities devoted to specific Wiccan traditions. Lurking in these spaces—provided that's permitted by the moderators—can be extremely informative. You'll slowly come to learn who takes issue with whom, and over time many of the most pressing controversies will recirculate in discussion. If the forum is particularly welcoming to seekers, it is also not inappropriate to ask polite questions, especially if you frame them in terms of "I'm trying to understand something so that I can respectfully pursue the tradition from an informed perspective." Be humble, and do more listening than speaking.

 FROM THE CIRCLE

People like to talk about each other, and Witches are no different. If you're lucky enough to find an outer court, then you'll hear a lot of this. Frequently, these stories are about the people closest to a coven—members, the parent coven, or the colorful and outspoken people in the local community. Whether these stories are funny, news about hard times, or the latest outrageous gossip, they serve an unstated deeper purpose. When Witches tell stories about one another, we're negotiating community values and borders—often unconsciously. Our arguments and controversies anchor our common identity, the authority of our elders, and the content of our tradition. Over time, these stories become history.

—*Lukaos, third degree high priest*

Lineage as a Magical Connection

Lineage is more than disagreements over traditional purity or fighting across individual lines. Fundamentally, it's about the passing of power, independent of any kind of wider social authority or concern over public scrutiny. When you belong to a Wiccan tradition, you are united by more than a shared Book of Shadows, a particular altar layout, or personal fondness. You are united through your upline to a communal body of power.

In the same way that a coven of committed members gradually builds its own egregore—its own personality or group mind, linking covenmates together on a magical level—a tradition gradually builds its own magical current. A Gardnerian circle for example, doesn't just *look* like a Gardnerian circle, it also *feels* like a Gardnerian circle. That feeling—that energy—is bigger than just the words of the rite or the individual tools that are used. Even if an outsider were to get ahold of a legitimate Gardnerian text and perform it to the letter, that feeling can't be replicated. Why? Because you can't fake the passing of real power. And this power is the most important component of lineage. It's more important than who initiated you, how long your training lasted, or whether or not anyone in your upline is still alive, years after the fact.

To continue with our doctor analogy, this is the ability to heal. A good medical school, a license, effective teachers, and diligent practice are critical, but these are not in and of themselves the power to cure illness and save lives. Belonging to a magical lineage is the ability to tap into that collective power, built up by generations of practitioners over time, working the same rituals, calling on the same entities, chanting the same words, carrying out the same traditions. The profound experiences that this generates—that *feeling* I described earlier—are one of Wicca's great Mysteries and can't be fairly put into words.

The idea that lineage is about the passing of a kind of power beyond the individuals involved has plenty of historical and religious precedent. Other occult groups have developed ideas about an inherent, collective essence that may be accessed upon initiation. We might also draw comparisons between Wiccan conceptions of lineage and certain Christian views of apostolic succession. Depending on perspective, that magical lineage may be strengthened and reinforced by its antiquity, its length, the power (and personalities) of the individuals who compose it, or the unique nature of the tradition being passed. It is difficult to make sweeping statements about what factors are inherently more meaningful than others. I have my own opinions, certainly, but as a seeker you may encounter many different perspectives. It's worth approaching all of them thoughtfully.

Uplines and Downlines

We usually speak of our lineages in terms of uplines and downlines. Imagine yourself standing in the middle of a vertical line. Your upline is the succession of Witches who have passed their tradition to you. This would normally include your initiating high priestess and high priest, the high priestess and high priest who initiated them, and so on. Some traditions trace the upline across the sexes, alternating male and female (so if you were a female initiate, you would trace your upline through the high priest that initiated you, and then through the high priestess that initiated him, etc.). Other traditions emphasize the high priestess alone, with both sexes tracing their lineage through a succession of women. As societal understandings of gender develop and nonbinary models become more common, many more variations are sure to exist.

Your downline, as you may have guessed, is made up of those Witches whom *you* have initiated, in accordance with whatever restrictions your specific tradition places on lineage (a man in a tradition that traces lineage through women, for example, may not, in the strictest sense, have a downline). If you have more than one initiate who then goes on to have their own initiates, your downline would come to be branched, like the familiar family tree diagram. If you belong to a tradition that traces lineage through *both* the high priestess and the high priest, your upline may be branched as well.

Uplines and downlines are important to traditional Wicca because they reinforce the practices and expectations of the tradition. Your upline is responsible for teaching, mentoring, and correcting as necessary. These are your elders, tasked with passing the tradition as it was passed to them. Their downline, in turn, commits to the same, should they have their own covens and initiates in time. As a group, their behavior and ultimate quality reflect back upon their upline, in the same way that a child's actions often tell us something about the nature of the parent. This creates a kind of social feedback that builds consistency in practice, preserving the individual tradition. One's upline and downline often come to function as and adopt the same language of family—a network of parents, grandparents, children, cousins, and siblings. Theoretically, you could begin with yourself and document a full family tree, back to the founders of your tradition and including every branch along the way, many lineages woven together into one coherent whole.

Vouching

So how do the members of any given tradition recognize each other? In the case of older kinds of Wicca, there may be so many initiates in different parts of the world that, not only could you probably not complete that full family tree, but you could certainly never know all of them personally. And yet initiates have ways of keeping track of each other, finding others, and distinguishing between themselves and outsiders. The most visible strategy—the one you're most likely to experience as you seek—is called vouching.

The premise of the vouching system is simple: given that initiation is a social process and a tradition is structured in terms of an interconnected series of lineages, everyone should have social and magical ties to someone else. One does not become a traditional Wiccan alone, after all. Vouching is the process by which one initiate affirms their connection with another. In doing so, others may more easily accept that person into their community:

"Yes, she's an initiate. I was at her elevation ritual."

"Yes, he's family. He and my coven sibling have circled together."

"Yes, let's invite them. I know their high priestess."

Vouching rarely happens in public space. If a new person appears on the scene and claims to be an initiate, the Wiccans in that community will likely have their own methods for evaluating that claim, and the newcomer may never even know. Alternatively, he may be asked to provide a vouch—the word of another known initiate in the community whom others know to be trustworthy. In whatever case, it should be clear that one cannot simply claim to be an initiate within a specific tradition without support and reasonably expect to be granted access to a private community. When I first began writing about Gardnerian Wicca online, I received several emails from all over the country asking who my high priestess was and whether or not I could supply the names of anyone who could second my claim of belonging. There was nothing rude or unexpected about these inquiries. I was online purporting to represent a community. It was only natural that the part of that community outside of my immediate family would ask for verification.

Traditional Wicca has a long history of outsiders pretending to be initiates. There is too much at stake to simply take the word of every person who makes the claim, especially if that person is recruiting for a coven, advertising themselves as a teacher (particularly one who charges a fee), or is otherwise trying to set themselves up as an authority. As a seeker, it is reasonable for you to ask around your communities, both in-person and online, to see if someone will vouch for a potential teacher or coven. Sadly, it is still a common occurrence that newcomers are duped by frauds. Sometimes, the best you'll be able to get is, "Yes, I know that person, and she's kind and well-informed." From there, you'll have to use your good sense and go with your gut. But we'll talk more about that in the next section!

Initiation and lineage are two of the most striking characteristics of traditional Wicca, separating it from most other kinds of contemporary Witchcraft and eclectic Wicca. These two concepts are closely linked but not interchangeable. Where initiation is the ritual act that marks a person as a member of the group, lineage is both the specific place of that person within it, as well as the magical connection that she shares with her upline and downline. Within a tradition, there may be many lines, and these often function as family groups, in which members build strong emotional ties, reinforcing a sense of loyalty amongst them.

Fundamentally, lineage is about belonging, which is a central, driving desire characteristic of the human experience. Whatever our communities, we want to feel like we belong somewhere—like we have a place in the world. Questions about lineage inspire heated controversy on all sides because they threaten that sense of belonging. When you encounter Witches who seem angry or frustrated when these issues arise, remember what feels at stake here for the people involved. The more secure you are in your own identity as a Witch, the less such controversies will rattle you. In the end, the support you receive through your lineage is inherently more important than what outsiders have to say about it.

FROM THE CIRCLE

When I think back to the time when I was a seeker, I remember occasionally thinking that if I found the right coven someday, it would be a wondrous utopia of spiritual people who have transcended most human faults and failings. This was in fact my own delusion in which I was placing unrealistic expectations on a future coven. If I did not transcend this fallacy, I would inevitably find disappointment in the end when I found out that each and every person makes mistakes.

Our coven brothers and sisters are learning just as we are. Today, as a coven leader, I learn something new each and every day. I feel that I must always remember to show humility in the way I lead within the coven in order to show that I am not infallible and that I, too, make many mistakes. What sets us all apart is whether we are willing to own up to those mistakes and if we have learned from them.

—*Thorn Nightwind, priest of the*
Horsa and Sacred Pentagraph traditions

CHAPTER 5

HIERARCHY

H ierarchy.
The word alone is enough to make some people cringe, if not immediately protest. It implies boundaries, oppression, power struggles, abuse, authority, and caste. For many, it triggers flashbacks to awful experiences in childhood religions. It may remind you of school, church, or government. "Hierarchy" speaks of corporate work environments, where creativity withers and bureaucracy robs workers of recourse and agency. "Hierarchy" is what keeps the social elite in power, lording over the impoverished masses.

And for all those reasons, it makes sense that it should give us pause. In so many ways, Wicca promises us freedom and independence and personal power—the chance to be who we really are. So what should we make of the role that hierarchy plays in its more traditional forms?

It often surprises seekers to learn that traditional Wicca is hierarchical. Most of the popular books available today emphasize the solitary practitioner, beholden to no one. She may explore to her heart's content, experimenting as she chooses, with nothing to stand in her way as she builds a unique, highly personalized practice. This is the Wicca that most newcomers first encounter. Even in groups, it is common to see more egalitarian structures. Members may take turns leading rituals or speak in terms of a shared learning experience; everyone is there to teach and to inspire everyone else. Such groups often eschew titles like "high priestess" or "high priest," except in token to whoever may be leading the night's activities.

In the seventies and eighties, many female-only covens (some identifying as Wiccan and many not) considered a coven hierarchy to be emblematic of a particular kind of patriarchal oppression, necessarily at odds with a feminist spiritual movement. The idea that someone might stand between a Witch and her gods—especially a Gerald Gardner or an Alex Sanders—wasn't just ludicrous, it was offensive. Indeed, it is this idea about "mediators" between an individual practitioner and the religious experience that is often the most problematic for seekers, especially those from authoritarian religious backgrounds.

But how does hierarchy actually function in traditional Wicca? Is it really as fraught as so many other kinds of Witches say? And why do we have it at all, given how poorly it seems to work out for so many in other settings?

I think it may be useful to start by giving you a window into my own preparations as a high priestess for a coven meeting. So often the focus is on the ritual itself, and seekers aren't given much insight into what goes on behind the curtain. I may be the leader of my coven, but that doesn't mean I can turn my initiates into servants or lord my magical prowess and infinite wisdom over them as though they were children begging for candy. Real leadership, as you'll see, is much less glamorous.

Hierarchy in Action

I pride myself on being a good housekeeper, generally, but even so there is a lot of work to do before people arrive for circle. I make sure things are put away, guest bedrooms are clean, tables are cleared, and the fridge is full. I vacuum all the floors and wipe down all the counters. I scrub the toilets and make sure the bathrooms are stocked with clean towels, toilet paper, and whatever else I think people may need. I ensure that we have all the ritual items we require. I buy or make the things that we don't have. My covenmates aren't guests in the usual sense; I don't wait on their every need or adhere to the typical social niceties that go along with inviting someone to your home for the first time. But I do want to make sure the space I present to them is clean and inviting. In exchange for my efforts (and, frankly, because I hate cooking) my initiates and students usually wrangle dinner. They also bring the ritual perishables: flowers for the altar, cookies or cakes to share during ritual, and a bottle of wine for libations. Who brings what rotates, and I prefer to be left out of the decision, because I'm already up to my elbows cleaning a toilet or a litter box.

This kind of ritualized reciprocity is important to us. Traditional Wiccan training cannot and should not be bought or sold (more on this in chapter 8), but there is nonetheless a practical cost involved. Time must be sacrificed and ritual supplies must be acquired. When I was a student traveling to my own high priestess's home, I coordinated food, wine, and flowers with my coven siblings. That gave our high priestess and high priest the freedom to focus on preparing their home and leading the ritual. Now, with my own coven, that's my job. Someday, my initiates will have their own covens and they will likely swap roles themselves.

Everyone pitching in like this ensures that no one person bears the brunt of the cost, in either time or money. It also creates a stronger sense of community. Everyone helps. Everyone is needed in order to build something precious.

Usually, my working partner and Foxfire's high priest, Lukaos, is first to arrive. We will have spoken on the phone several times beforehand, but we nonetheless spend some time before others arrive figuring out what needs to be done that night. We discuss how our initiates and students are progressing. We come up with strategies to help them individually. Is there something we need to discuss privately with Corvus? Could Lore use a personalized project? Is there something we need to make sure to cover in circle? We've been known to rehearse difficult conversations before we have them with people. We also spend a lot of time sharing our own personal experiences and thoughts, giving each other feedback on how those may be impacting our interactions with our covenmates. We swap family gossip, insights from things we've read lately, and we decide what may be worth sharing with the whole coven. Then, of course, we do whatever finalizing or practicing the evening's ritual may require.

As people arrive, we prepare food, catch up, foster discussion, and work with individuals as necessary. A lot of forethought goes into the decisions we make here. Even in a shared tradition, everyone's path in the Craft is totally their own. Our initiates are all in different places. They come in with different experiences and different needs. There's no prepackaged curriculum for training Witches or passing our tradition. In many ways, these moments before the actual ritual are some of the most critical. Bonds are forged and cemented, oral lore is passed, lessons are learned, and secrets are shared. And all before the circle is even cast!

After everyone has eaten and dishes have been put away, Lukaos and I sequester ourselves and prepare for ritual. While we do that, everyone else sets up the space. They assemble the altar, make sure wine and cookies are plated and ready for libating, and, of course, they prepare themselves in whatever manner they need, all with senior members guiding newcomers as necessary.

This is hierarchy in action.

As a high priestess, my authority is not some inborn, divinely gifted power that entitles me to boss other people around. This isn't power for the sake of power, designed to keep people in their place so I can feel important and special. My authority is neither domineering, nor is it arbitrary. It's born out of the fact that I have experience that my students simply do not.

I'm transmitting something to them that can only be achieved by actually *doing* things, not reading about them or imagining them with other beginners. A traditional coven is hierarchical in the same way that a classroom is hierarchical. As a schoolteacher (which is really what I do for a living), I'm not in charge of my classroom because of some innate specialness. I'm in charge because I've got years of education and specialized training that my students simply don't have. If I do my job, they'll go on to acquire all of that in time. No teacher wants to keep her students in the same classroom year after year. Likewise, Wiccan initiates are expected to progress, building the skills of priests and priestesses in their own right and ultimately becoming autonomous (and maybe becoming coven leaders themselves). Continuing with our classroom analogy, we may employ a variety of educational models. Some teachers simply give lectures and require students to keep up. Others rely on more student-centered strategies, letting individuals explore according to their own learning styles. But no matter how progressive and experimental the classroom, there is still hierarchy in place. That hierarchy is based on the fact that the teacher is the one with the content to be disseminated, as well as the skill to transfer it effectively.

Note how, in my example, increased experience brings increased authority. Lukaos shares some of my leadership responsibilities because he, too, has that experience. Initiates who have been around longer assist those who are newer. The degree system is a way of measuring this kind of progress and maturity. Ideally, a degree system reflects experience; it shouldn't be taken as a statement about inherent personal value, nor is it a license to push people around just because you need to feel like you're better than someone else. The goal is to build people up, not keep them underneath you.

Part of my authority also comes out of the role that I play as host. I take on the responsibility of providing a safe, clean space for my coven. I organize schedules, orchestrate rituals, and provide the necessary working tools. I put in most of the time required to do these things, as is the responsibility of a good host. Guests, in turn, have their own responsibilities, particularly respect and courtesy. All the rules of good manners apply. If any of my covenmates desired more decision-making power, they could consider taking on the role of host. Put plainly, if you want to be in charge of a coven, you have to put in the work of starting, housing, and facilitating that coven! It's an enormous job. Often, the egalitarian model comes out of the desire to avoid burdening one person with the task. Many other kinds of covens fall apart simply because no one wants to do the mundane labor of running one. Traditional Wiccan coven leaders are prepared over time and adhere to certain protocols and preexisting structures (such as an established liturgy), which make things less overwhelming than they might be otherwise.

Lukaos and I didn't simply wake up one day, declare ourselves lords of the realm, and start advertising for peons. Honestly, the process of hiving and assuming leadership roles was a fraught one. We spent a lot of time asking ourselves why anyone would follow us anywhere and what we really had to offer. We may not have done it at all had it not been for our first seeker, Corvus, who began pursuing training from me when I was still a fresh second degree. I told her no more than once, for different reasons. I was too inexperienced. I was too busy. I didn't have a working partner yet. It really should be a group effort, not just me with one student. On and on. Corvus's persistence was finally rewarded after a second seeker showed up—Lore—and the two ganged up on me. I no longer felt like I could say no.

But that didn't make me an automatic expert, and I refused to put up a front for them. Even once I was elevated to third degree, I understood that there's a lot of mileage between the ritual afterglow and the tempered wisdom of elderhood. I was no elder, and I told them so. I opened my doors and took on the role of high priestess with the understanding that my job would be to teach them what it meant to be priestesses of my tradition, and that I would screw up sometimes. I can only ever teach what I know and offer what experience I have. What I wouldn't do, I told them, was be their mother, their foreman, or their therapist. I'm not any of those things. As a third degree, I had made a commitment to my gods and to my community, and all I could do was show them how and why I did those things. If other people felt called to this as I did, I could show them the way as it was shown to me. I wouldn't be a mediator between them and the gods; I would simply model the techniques for reaching those gods *so that they could do so themselves*. In turn, they would respect that experience. If they had felt they could do it on their own, presumably they wouldn't have asked me to begin with. Should they change their minds, they could leave at any time.

Just like in a healthy classroom run by an experienced teacher, the goal is reciprocity. I bring my experience and the content I have to offer, and my students bring the willingness to learn. It's not their responsibility to feed my ego or obey my every whim. If anything, my real position in the hierarchy is the one of service. My initiates don't serve me; I serve them. I may be the high priestess, and I may call most of the shots, but I'm also the one cleaning the toilets.

The Purpose of Hierarchy

In discussing hierarchy as it actually looks in a real coven setting, its purpose should be clearer. The degree system isn't license to bully lower ranking members, and the high priestess and high priest aren't there to stand between you and the gods like self-righteous gatekeepers. Instead, the coven hierarchy is in place to facilitate learning. Much of the liturgy, history, lore, and techniques of magical practice are transmitted by tier and accompanied by oaths of secrecy. Some materials are only appropriate for third degrees. Others are available to all initiates equally. Some materials only make sense for those running covens. Still more are most meaningful for working couples. Everything exists within a wider context, and some pieces of any tradition will naturally hold greater Mystery for some and not others, at various points in their lives and practices. Further, turning again to our school analogy, some materials build upon others, essentially creating prerequisites. A rite may make no sense without first considering another, so a coven leader may choose to introduce them in succession. It's worth spending time processing certain lessons before moving on or taking on additional complexity. An elevation represents preparedness to move forward, though the criteria will vary across covens.

A hierarchical system will usually apply to the entire tradition, at least theoretically. We generally have a sense that first degrees are relatively inexperienced, and that third degrees warrant some level of additional respect, but the reality is that each individual coven sets its own expectations and standards. A first degree in my coven isn't automatically entitled to the same privileges as a first degree in another coven, especially in another tradition. Similarly, the high priestess of a coven can't just show up at a public gathering and reasonably expect people outside of that coven to start deferring to her or calling her by whatever titles she may have earned. Hierarchy stops functioning outside of context.

Hierarchy is also a test of commitment, functioning to protect the larger interests of a wider tradition. Bringing someone into the inner sanctum of a coven is an act of deep trust. An outer court and a degree system allow this process to occur gradually, with the new Witch building stronger relationships within the coven and experience enough to handle the weight of added responsibility. Strong partnerships of any kind usually take significant amounts of time to develop. Romantic relationships rarely begin with marriage vows. Similarly, commitment to a particular tradition usually comes about in stages, designed to ensure that all parties involved make informed decisions.

On a magical level, organizing training in these kinds of stages better prepares neophyte Witches for more advanced work. Just like in a conventional classroom, some material must build on prior knowledge. The degree system is one way that we measure (albeit imperfectly) that preparedness to receive and process more complex material, or else to put familiar material together in novel, more profound ways. In working through a particular degree—however long it may take—an initiate primes herself to advance as a Witch, beyond just earning a title. In this way, Wiccan hierarchy is much more akin to something like a guild system than a caste system. The initiate displays mastery over time, thus earning the right to progress and perhaps one day to take on students of their own.

The reality, too, is that traditional Wicca has a lengthy history of attracting people with less than sincere intentions. It seems to just generally be true of people: when you've got a secret, other people will go out of their way to find it out. There have been many seekers over the years, in practically any tradition you could name, who've only stuck around long enough (and put on a good enough face) to be initiated and gain access to some Book of Shadows or other. Listen long enough to any elder in any tradition, and you'll hear a story about some oathbreaker from days past who got initiated, published secret materials, left to start their own tradition with stolen rituals, or some such. Tales of infiltrating journalists and academics abound, just out for a sexy story. Also prevalent are cautionary tales about sexual predators, Witches from other covens with nefarious intentions, and other more dramatic characters. Put it all on paper, and it starts sounding paranoid and melodramatic.

Except that all of these things have actually happened.

Just recently came the publication of Alex Mar's *Witches of America* (2015), which sparked outrage from members of the Feri tradition of Witchcraft (an initiatory, non-Wiccan form of Craft with a similar emphasis on secrecy), amongst others. Mar, a journalist, gained access to several Witch and other occult communities, and, whether her intentions were ill or not, much of what she learned and saw ended up in a popular book, allegedly without the consent of the Witches she had befriended and with whom she had studied and ultimately practiced Craft.

This sort of thing happens all the time, in one way or another. Sometimes, it's a far-reaching violation, like the publication of a revealing book or article.[12] Other times, it's an ill-trained, careless first

---

12. Alex Mar's *Witches of America* is only one example of this phenomenon, which may constitute its own genre. Another notable title is Tanya Luhrmann's *Persuasions of the Witch's Craft: Ritual Magic in Contemporary England* (1989).

degree who simply makes a mistake on a public forum, sharing material that they shouldn't. Tiered training ensures that only *fragments* of a coven's rites and lore risk inappropriate exposure should we make mistakes about the people we choose to include.

 FROM THE CIRCLE

Most Wiccan Elders are more than willing to share with a sincere seeker. You may decide that initiation is not right for you in their tradition, but the friendships formed can be beautiful and long-lasting. Most Wiccan Elders are willing to teach their religion to sincere and dedicated seekers, but it seems that there are a lot of seekers who don't ask them for one reason or another. The seeker may not know they can ask them or they may feel they don't know enough to ask. As a coven leader, I will not have all the answers they may be looking for, but I will do my best to answer to the best of my ability. When you question, I may question you back in order to challenge you to dig deep within, study, and ferret out the answers so that you can draw your own conclusions at times. Your answer will be more important than mine. But don't be afraid to ask for help in the first place! The worst anyone can do is say no.

—*Thorn Nightwind, priest of the*
Horsa and Sacred Pentagraph traditions

When Hierarchy Goes Wrong

One pervasive misconception about traditional Wicca is that it's all about letting yourself be pushed around by some high muckety-muck, who promises you power and belonging but really just takes advantage of your naïveté and sincerity. I hope I've already disabused you of that, but stereotypes and misunderstandings can be very persistent. Traditional Wicca has been around for at least three-quarters of a century, and in that time there have been plenty of people burned by other people's power trips. Horror stories range from being ripped off financially by some self-declared Wiccan teacher, to sexual abuse at the hands of an initiator, to just being bullied by a coven bent on convincing you that if you don't do things their way, then you're not fit to be part of the Craft at all. Witches of any kind tend to be extremely independent people, so the thought of being beholden to anyone else's rules is pretty hard to stomach for most of us. And all of those horror stories of power abuse have to come from somewhere, right?

It's true that there's plenty of room for Wiccan hierarchy to go wrong. The fact of the matter is that any time you have people operating in groups, not everyone is going to play by the rules. This is as true about professional organizations, athletic teams, and parent-teacher associations as it is about Wiccans. While generally I believe in the goodness of human beings, some people are selfish, destructive, abusive, or power hungry. There are absolutely people in the world who don't have your best interests at heart, and some of those people are your fellow Witches. Rather than telling you that it doesn't happen or putting a bag over my head and declaring that *real* Wiccans would never do such things (there are duds in every community, and we don't get to just disown them to avoid having hard conversations), I think it's more useful to discuss how to recognize and avoid the kinds of covens and teachers that pose these risks. We'll do that at length in section three. For now, a good rule of thumb is this: you're a grown-up. No one else gets to tell you how to live, how to spend your money, who to have sex with (or to have sex at all), or what to think. People may offer advice, caution you one way or another, or even pressure you and deliver ultimatums, for good or ill. But *you* are in charge of making your own decisions. No one else's occult titles or years of experience can take that away from you.

The relationship between a high priestess or high priest and their initiates does represent a difference in authority, it's true, but *only within that coven and that tradition*. You never give up your individual power, which you acquired just by becoming an adult in the world. You can walk away from any coven at any time. You can say no. You can absolutely look for another coven or teacher that will support the choices you know are best for you. As you seek, take the time to periodically remind yourself of this reality.

CHAPTER 6
EXPERIENCE

I'm interested in learning more about Wicca. Can you tell me what Wiccans believe?"

It sounds like a simple question. It's certainly a common one. Scan the Pagan or Witchcraft pages of any popular online forum and you'll see it repeated dozens of times, at least. This is also the most commonly posed question from curious outsiders. Whether you're beginning a conversation with a family member or participating in some kind of media interview or academic survey, that first question is very likely going to be, "What do you believe?"

This is the question we're used to asking when approaching a religion for the first time. Want to know about Buddhism? Catholicism? Islam? There's a good chance you'll start with belief. In many parts of the world, especially North America and Western Europe, we tend to think that religion is fundamentally about the things we think. Religion is largely internal, made up of beliefs, which we use to create rules, which in turn dictate our lifestyle choices. This understanding of religion, however, is actually quite narrow. Thanks to a lengthy and sordid history of imperialism—especially Christian imperialism—we collectively tend to expect "religion" to look like a particular kind of Christianity (and Protestantism, in particular).[13] That's become our

---

13. For more, consider Tomoko Masuzawa's *The Invention of World Religion* (Chicago: University of Chicago Press, 2005).

prototype, and it's happened so subtly and for so long that most of us don't even notice it. We just think that's what religion *is*. A "real" religion has beliefs, creeds, sacred texts, and specialized clergy that provide public services (like weddings and funerals). "Real" religion concerns itself with the afterlife and morality. In both the academic study of religion and in popular conversation, we've even come to use particularly Christian terms—faith, church, minister, seminary—as though they are totally neutral and applicable to all traditions. This is part of the reason why Pagans now have seminaries and Wiccans sometimes feel compelled to "baptize" their children in rituals called Wiccanings. And, because belief is so central to most kinds of Protestantism—and our understanding of religion as a phenomenon comes from the emphasis we've historically placed on Protestantism—that's usually where we think we need to start.

"Well, what do members of that religion believe?" In other words, how does this unfamiliar religion compare to Protestantism?

Over and over, usually without our awareness. So what happens when *belief* isn't central to the religion in question? What do we do when "religion" doesn't look how we expect it to?

Most of the time, we end up having an argument over whether or not what we're discussing is a religion at all. We hedge our bets and say things like, "Well, it's really more of a philosophy than a religion" or "This is more about spirituality than religion." Increasingly, we describe ourselves as "spiritual but not religious," because somewhere along the line we decided that "religious" meant being close-minded, old-fashioned, or obsessed with dogma. Rather than challenging ourselves to adopt a different approach to religion, we simply find a different word. It's a lot easier to just call something a "lifestyle" or a "philosophy" than it is to question our cultural attitudes about religion as a category; they're so ingrained that we don't even realize that we're biased, let alone understand where those biases originated.

The result of that kind of intellectual laziness is that we hamper our own understanding when we try to learn about a tradition that doesn't match our limited prototypes. In order to better understand traditional Wicca, we have to disabuse ourselves of the notion that religion is all about what people *believe.*

Consider our earlier conversations about the characteristics of traditional Wicca that I've described so far: the significance of the coven, the centrality of initiation, the emphasis on lineage, and the function of hierarchy. Those things are primarily about what people *do.* They may imply certain beliefs (particularly about relationships and certainly about magic), but many of those heavy issues we usually associate with religion—the nature of the gods, the afterlife, issues of morality, good and evil—are left to the individual Witch. Those are Mysteries that many prefer to approach alone, or in the intimate comfort of our covens. Many of us wouldn't be able to express these things adequately in words even if we tried. Some of us look to reason, others to gut feeling. Still more retain beliefs from prior socialization and religious upbringing. In any case, we arrive by different means. Conversations about these topics can and certainly do take place in wider circles within whole traditions, but there is no ultimate, holy authority who dictates what an individual Witch must think. No high priest or high priestess can see into your mind and perfectly ascertain your beliefs. They can only measure you by your actions, so it is by our actions that we recognize each other.

Orthodoxy versus Orthopraxy

As you're exploring traditional Wicca, you may hear practitioners explain their personal practice in terms of "orthodoxy" and "orthopraxy." These terms have long been used in formal academic spaces, especially within fields like anthropology and religious studies, but they're becoming increasingly common in casual conversation, too. They're a bit more complicated than people usually make them sound, however. Strictly speaking, "orthopraxy" derives from Greek and means "right practice." In usage, it stands in contrast to "orthodoxy," which means "right belief." Orthodoxy has been used in

Christian spaces to indicate that believers adhere to specific doctrines established in the days of the early church. Though historically various groups have differed about exactly which doctrines comprise a truly orthodox (and therefore "correct") Christianity, what is central, for our purposes, is that it is *belief* that is the concern. A religious group collectively makes a statement about the nature of reality—for example, that Jesus Christ is both fully God and fully man—and individuals either adhere to this now-established piece of dogma (what we might simply understand as "truth"), or they reject it in favor of other, dissenting beliefs (what many Christians would call "heresy").

Orthodoxy is concerned with the adherence to established beliefs. Belongingness is determined primarily by sharing opinions, thoughts, and stated truths. For more popular forms of Wicca—what we've come to call eclectic Wicca—this usually means that members are expected to express belief in various tenets. This frequently includes the Wiccan Rede ("An it harm none, do as ye will"), the Threefold Law (the belief that the good or ill you do in the world returns to you threefold), a belief in the inherent holiness of the natural world, and a paired goddess and god whose central myth is embodied in a particular seasonal cycle. If someone were to call themselves Wiccan but then follow that up by stating that they didn't believe in these things, we would probably question whether or not they were truly Wiccan, in the popular sense of the term. An eclectic Wiccan might never cast a spell or conduct a formal ritual, but as long as she lived according to the rede and professed belief in the Goddess, she would likely still be accepted as Wiccan in eclectic communities. This is a more orthodoxic view of Wicca—it's what you believe, think, and feel that's ultimately important.

In contrast is "orthopraxy"—right practice. Orthopraxic traditions emphasize action. Belonging is marked by what people actually do, not by what they think or believe. A more orthopraxic religion would be less invested in whether or not members shared a particular perspective. What matters instead is the practice itself (the performance of specific rituals, the presence of particular social structures, and the consistency of particular behaviors amongst members). Traditional Wicca tends toward orthopraxy. Belief is not enough. You cannot simply think or feel a certain way. It's not a matter of reading about certain ideas and holding them to be true in your heart. An orthopraxic perspective demands that adherents take action. For traditional Wicca, that means performing the rites of the tradition.

And if that sounds too simple, it's because it is! It has become relatively common to hear traditional Wiccan practitioners say things like, "Wicca is an orthopraxic religion, not an orthodoxic religion. It's not about what you believe." Such a statement, while potentially useful for understanding how the practitioner views his own Craft, is really only partially true. The reality is that, outside of theoretical categorization, orthopraxy and orthodoxy are neither discrete nor are they mutually exclusive. Belief and practice are intimately linked things, as one implies the other. What we think and how we feel tend to drive us to action. Meanwhile our practices suggest underlying beliefs. Action fosters emotions and opinions, while also reinforcing worldviews, even when it does so unconsciously. "Orthopraxic" and "orthodoxic" make convenient categories for religion scholars, and they do represent a legitimate difference in emphasis for many kinds of Wiccans, but we shouldn't understand them in overly concrete terms. It's not that traditional Wiccans are totally devoid of belief; it's that their criteria for membership rests upon action—initiation, the practice of particular rites, organization into a hierarchical coven, the passing of lineage—rather than a particular internal vision about the nature of the world and our relationship with it.

An Experiential Religion

While it may be fair to observe that traditional Wicca tends toward orthopraxy, it is more consistently true to say that traditional Wicca is *experiential*. By and large, we believe (there I go again with belief) that our Craft must be experienced firsthand in order to really be understood. Further, these experiences—particularly those that are consistent for individuals within a single tradition—cannot be clearly expressed to someone who hasn't shared in them. There's something about the Mysteries that transcends language, or so practitioners often insist. In short, traditional Wicca isn't something you can simply read about. It's not just something you believe in. It's something that you *do*.

Fundamentally, the process of training in a coven is designed to build experience. Without dictating what an initiate must believe about the gods, coven leaders create the space (both physically and magically) for initiates to encounter the gods on their own terms. The boundaries of tradition serve as scaffolding for a personal experience of the Craft. As we discussed in our look at hierarchy, the task of the high priestess or high priest is not to serve as a mediator between you and the divine—it's to help you build that connection for yourself. The bonds that you will forge, the experiences you'll share, the epiphanies you'll have, and the challenges you'll face are not the sorts of things that you can simulate through reading or observing. You have to physically and emotionally engage in the *doing* of Witchcraft. Solitary practice and eclectic practice provide their own unique experiences, which are also valuable. They are, however, distinct experiences. One is not a substitute for the other.

When other kinds of Witches and occultists insist that traditional forms of Wicca are outdated or otherwise less valid because so much of Wicca has been publicized, what they're really doing is failing to understand the value of that firsthand experience. I once sat through a conversation at a Pagan meetup in which a local leader—who had no idea I was a Gardnerian priestess—explained to us that traditional Wicca was obsolete because, to quote, "It's all on the internet now, anyway." The people around me nodded sagely, as though congratulating themselves for not wasting their time pursuing something that they could simply Google in an afternoon. I sipped my coffee and remained silent, wondering what their own practices must be like that they felt like mine could be reduced to something pasted on a sacred texts website. How impoverished must their own Craft be that they couldn't recognize oversimplification and incompleteness (not to mention downright lies) when they saw it? Oh well.

It's true that there's been a lot of material published in various media over the last several decades purportedly from traditional sources. The fact is, eclectic Wicca had to come from a place, and that place is largely traditional Wiccan lore made available through the spread of the Pagan Way and other outer court materials, tabloid exposés, revealing academic texts, and rogue initiates out to scandalize their teachers and build a name for themselves. Some of that material is more misleading than helpful, or else it's so devoid of its original context that it's practically meaningless. In any case, what all of it is missing is the nuance of practical experience within the intended, structured environment provided by a healthy coven. Part of the intention behind traditional hierarchy is the preparation of the individual Witch to receive the Mysteries through direct experience. This is a process that goes beyond simple exposure to a text.

Dion Fortune (1890–1946), a famous British occultist and prolific writer known for her work in the Fraternity of the Inner Light, believed that mystical information could only be understood by those who were ready to receive it. It didn't matter if a student was accidentally exposed to secret materials (and Fortune herself was accused of breaking her own oaths by publishing certain information in her books; she had a lot to say regarding the role of secrecy in occult traditions), because it simply wouldn't be meaningful. A magician who wasn't ready to learn would not be able to retain the information, anyway. Wisdom would take hold in the consciousness, slowly growing like a seed, but only with care. Without that, it would simply fail to take root.[14]

---

14. Dion Fortune, *The Mystical Qabalah*, rev. ed. (1935; repr., San Francisco: Red Wheel/Weiser, 2000), 27–33, 85–86.

Personally, I think there's some merit to this, though my reasoning is a little more mundane: out of context, things tend to just not make as much sense. Further, if you haven't put the work into achieving something on a deep emotional and spiritual level (if you haven't *worked* for something), it won't hold value for you.

Let's go back to our imaginary high priestess Glinda and her flying cats, whom we met in chapter 4. In order to progress in Glinda's tradition of Flying Cat Wicca, initiates put in years of hard work. They attend weekly coven meetings and develop personal practices at home. They spend a lot of time discussing their history, the reasoning behind their rites, and how they personally connect to them. They share a massive body of oral lore, which is always growing, developing, and deepening. Individual Flying Cat Wiccans build intimate relationships with their gods, whom they come to love in a way that isn't really possible to explain to outsiders, even when they try. Covens are like families, and every time they're visited by Flying Cat Wiccans from other regions, they learn something new about their own Craft.

Now imagine that a portion of Glinda's personal copy of the Flying Cat Tradition's Book of Shadows ends up on the internet. It's not really clear how it got there. Perhaps Glinda made one of her initiates upset and they wanted to take some kind of grade school–level revenge. Or maybe the person who posted it was genuinely acting selflessly, believing that such sacred information should be available to everyone indiscriminately, like a modern-day Prometheus (Pro*meow*theus?) bringing fire to humanity. Maybe it's just one ritual, or maybe it's the entirety of the book as it's given to new initiates. Whatever.

Are the people reading it online going to have the same appreciation as the people who are members of Glinda's coven? They have the ritual (or maybe more), sure. They also have some strangers on the internet insisting that the material is genuine (because, as we all know, if it's on the internet it's definitely true). They can read the words and even try adapting things on their own.

But they are not sharing in the *experience* of being an initiate. They are not *earning* that material. They are not privy to the *context* of that material, nor do they have access to the oral lore and the years of personal and magical development required to grasp what's really going on. The experience of working in a coven, being initiated into a tradition, and training to progress as a Witch within a specific system cannot be simulated through reading. Even if you stumbled upon genuine oathbound material, it would necessarily be incomplete. The value lies in the process itself, and access to that can only ever be earned.

 FROM THE CIRCLE

At the age of forty, within the period of a month, I had an enormous paradigm shift from a very secular nonmagical worldview to acknowledging that I was an animist (of some sort), to realizing I wanted, more than anything, to be a lineaged Witch. When I got word back that I would be invited to an outer court circle, I had this really strange, intense fight-or-flight response. Part of me wanted to call the high priestess back and say, "No, never mind, I change my mind!" And part of me was thrilled beyond words and floating on cloud nine. The funny thing is, in the weeks leading up to initiation, I experienced this volley of emotions. It was a real and fundamentally deep change for me, a seeming antithesis to everything I had done or believed for the previous twenty years of my life (really, my entire adult life).

—*Wren, first degree priestess*

What about Ethics?

I can hear the protests already.

What about the Wiccan Rede! What about the Threefold Law! What about loving nature and honoring the divine feminine! Surely these things are fundamental to Wicca! How can you not include these in any kind of discussion about what Wicca is or is not?

So often the rede and the Threefold Law are discussed as the cornerstones of Wiccan identity—for many in eclectic communities and in wider Pagan circles, these are what *makes* someone Wiccan—and it feels almost like blasphemy to leave them out. How many other kinds of Witches have you known who started out pursuing Wicca but stopped because they were told that Wicca wouldn't allow them to practice baneful or defensive magic? That every action they made would return threefold? That only environmentalists and vegetarians and Democrats could be Wiccan? That being Wiccan entails promoting a particular understanding of karma and a seemingly impossible moral absolute about never doing harm?

These are stereotypes, certainly, but they come from somewhere. For decades, eclectic forms of Wicca—just by virtue of being more numerous—have defined the whole movement according to a particular vision popularized as the end of the twentieth century approached. In 1974, the American Council of Witches, a short-lived group consisting of numerous prominent Pagan leaders, articulated the "Principles of Wiccan Belief." This list of thirteen statements defined a worldview that members hoped would foster unity and lend respectability to Paganism as a world religion. In particular, the "Principles of Wiccan Belief" emphasized the centrality of nature and the importance of attaining harmony with the natural world, further codifying an environmental ethic that had become key to many Pagan traditions. They also decried the worship of the devil and the attainment of power at the expense of others. The Principles circulated widely into the early 2000s—there would even be subsequent attempts to revive the council—and new generations of seekers came to accept them, or variations on them, as given. Meanwhile, most of the books widely available to Wiccan seekers promoted solitary, eclectic practice and heavily emphasized a particular brand of morality rooted in a particular interpretation of tenets—particularly the Wiccan Rede and the Threefold Law—that had been circulating in Witchcraft communities in various forms for many decades.

There is still a great deal of debate surrounding both the origins and meaning of both the rede and the Threefold Law. Certainly, early Wiccans were, like many European spiritual seekers of the time, enamored with a romanticized version of the East rooted in colonialism. The concept of karma—in which one's actions in this life are thought to impact future lives in the cycle of rebirth—became increasingly commonplace. As Wiccans entered into public life for the first time after the publication of Gerald Gardner's books (and others shortly thereafter), there was also pressure to appear benign to concerned onlookers. Many Wiccans were very invested in promoting their religion as "white Witchcraft," focusing on healing, self-development, and otherwise doing good in the world (remember, there were still laws against Witchcraft in place in some regions). Gardner himself described a Wiccan ethic that came to serve as a predecessor to the now-popular Rede:

> [Witches] are inclined to the morality of the legendary Good King Pausol, "Do what you like so long as you harm no one." But they believe a certain law to be important, "You must not use magic for anything which will cause harm to anyone, and if, to prevent a greater wrong being done, you must discommode someone, you must do it only in a way which will abate the harm." [15]

It was important for the burgeoning new religion to put suspicious outsider minds at ease. And many of these early Wiccans surely believed in this moral imperative and sought to reverse what they saw as Witch stereotypes. They were vocal about their belief in consequences for the working of negative magic, and insisted that true Witches never sought to do evil. Doreen Valiente reiterated much of this in her own writing, including in a piece titled "The Witches' Creed" in her

---

15. Gerald Gardner, *The Meaning of Witchcraft* (York Beach, ME: Red Wheel/Weiser, 2004), 108.

book *Witchcraft for Tomorrow* (1978). Valiente—as well as later Wiccan writers—sought to build connections between this Wiccan morality and earlier codes of behavior, including the teachings of Saint Augustine, who instructed early Christians to, "Love and do what you want." [16] In doing so, Wicca could more effectively garner respectability in mainstream circles. This was a moral religion, like any other! As Wicca spread and new forms developed, these tenets were further codified in popular books for beginners and in popular discourse within Pagan communities.

Though the Wiccan Rede and Threefold Law have so long been promoted as universalities—essential beliefs that define all Wiccan practitioners—this has never *actually* been the case (and much of this has been the work of practitioners outside of the older initiatory systems). Variations have always existed, and even the word "rede" itself means "advice" or "counsel," not command. Individual covens have the freedom to practice as they deem appropriate, and the exact nature and specific contents of the various Books of Shadows are, to this day, secret. To assert that they share a common, codified morality is folly. I do not presume to know the intimacies of other covens—particularly in other traditions—and find it laughable that any could presume to know mine.

As you seek, expect to encounter a great deal of variety. Individual practitioners may hold a number of ethical positions. They may come from different backgrounds and hold different values. Often, their upbringings, regional origins, and life experiences will have as much (and probably more) bearing on their personal codes of conduct and the way in which they interact with the world as a Wiccan. Wiccans raised in politically liberal California will likely hold different beliefs from those born in the American South. Wiccan military veterans often hold different perspectives on war and bloodshed than those with

---

16. Augustine, *Homilies on the First Epistle of John*, ed. Daniel E. Doyle and Thomas Martin (New York: New City Press, 2008), 110.

pacifist backgrounds. "Harm none" may mean something different to a sheltered suburban teenager than to an adult living amidst urban poverty. A victim of domestic violence may have different opinions regarding the consequences of baneful magic than someone who has lived in safety all her life. And every one of these may represent a Wiccan perspective. It is that personal experience—coupled with the individuality emphasized by Wiccan practice—that informs one's personal code of ethics. Even when we use the Wiccan Rede or Threefold Law as a framework, no two Witches will do so in quite the same way.

There's a lot of overlap between religious belief and religious experience. It's really not helpful to be strict in the boundaries that we draw, as though one exists independently of the other. Our beliefs inform our practice, and our experience within that practice alters our beliefs. One isn't truly separate from the other. The issue is simply that, culturally, when we're talking about religion, we tend to emphasize belief at the expense of all else. Traditional Wicca often throws seekers (and scholars) for a loop because our focus is practice and the experience of the individual. We don't necessarily share an ethical code or an understanding of the exact nature of the divine. We don't all have the same relationship with nature or with the rest of the world at large. Our backgrounds, our unique covens and traditions, and our direct contact with the divine (as it appears to each of us individually) make our Witchcraft difficult to define in the manner of so many other religions. Our boundaries are constructed based on what members *do*, rather than what they believe. Remember, this is called a "Craft" for a reason. We recognize other practitioners by the actions they perform. We define individual traditions by the specific rites that they perform and the manner in which they organize their groups, not by their thoughts and feelings. In the same manner that we recognize a blacksmith by his practice of smithing, we recognize a Witch by his practice of Witchcraft. The emotions, theologies, and reasonings behind that Witchcraft may vary significantly, even within the same coven. The *experience* of Witchcraft may be unique to each practitioner, but that experience is what sets us apart.

Traditional Wicca is not the Wicca that circulates so freely on most bookshelves and internet forums. The importance of the coven dynamic, the formal initiation into the tradition, the passing of lineage, and the functions of hierarchy and personal experience all make traditional Wicca considerably different from the many other kinds of Witchcraft available to the contemporary seeker. Now that we've considered these five central components of traditional Wicca in depth, it's time to get to the real business of seeking. In the following section, we'll look at the process of actually finding a coven and contacting its leaders (and persuading them to give you a shot!). We'll also consider some of the pitfalls that go along with being a seeker, including how to figure out what you *really* need from a coven, recognizing red flags, and what to expect from traditional training.

 FROM THE CIRCLE

My personal ethical code comes not only from my upbringing, but also from the practice of traditional Wicca itself. In 1971, Sybil Leek published her classic book on Witchcraft called *The Complete Art of Witchcraft*. In the book, she details what have become known as the "Eight Tenets of Witchcraft." These include living a balanced life, humility, reincarnation, love, trust, humility, tolerance, and learning. To me, these eight tenets lay out ideals that we can strive for and directly add to the personal ethical code that I was raised with.

I also work toward ideals that I learn through the celebration of the sabbat festivals. Originally, there were only four seasonal rituals, but today we have eight sabbats, and each strives to teach us its own unique lessons. Even when a full coven of Witches has attended the same sabbat festival, each Witch will leave the ritual with their own observations, perspectives, and interpretation. What they get out of the ritual depends on what they need to learn from it at that time.

> —*Thorn Nightwind, priest of the*
> *Horsa and Sacred Pentagraph traditions*

PART III
SEEKING TRADITIONAL WICCA

CHAPTER 7
FINDING A COVEN

"Well, here we go," I muttered to myself, finally hitting the send button after several minutes of staring at the email I'd spent too much time composing. I was nervous, loosened by an extra glass of wine, and figured that I really didn't have anything to lose at this point. I'd begun practicing eclectic Wicca when I was fourteen. In college, I'd been a member of a grove in Blue Star Wicca. I'd explored non-Wiccan forms of Witchcraft after that. I'd been to more open rituals and Pagan meetups than I could remember (and plenty I wished I could forget). I'd started book clubs, attended student groups in college, and even been dedicated into a coven that had turned out to not be quite the right fit. I was done.

When I first started exploring Wicca as a young teenager, I'd been intrigued by the stories I read about the older traditions. What must it have been like, in Wicca's early days, to belong to a coven and practice oathbound magic rites in total secrecy? *I wish people still did things that way*, I thought, dreaming fervently that I was part of something that powerful.

Of course, they did. They do. But for some reason—maybe it was the books I was reading, or maybe it was the people I was hanging out with—I got it into my head that these older ways had died out, replaced by new, more correct, "progressive" kinds of Witchcraft that people found more fulfilling or more authentic. Why be bossed around by a high priestess when you could be your *own* high priestess? Why not forge your own way and build your *own* tradition? No one could say who was and who wasn't *really* a Wiccan! It had been decades, and we were a new generation with different needs and different experiences!

But part of me still longed for the romance that I experienced the first time I read Doreen Valiente and Gerald Gardner. When I looked at those old black and white photographs of Patricia Crowther, Janet Farrar, and Maxine Sanders, I felt something stir in my *bones*. After all these years and every experience I'd had in hundreds of other circles, a part of me never forgot that I had longed for whatever *that* was. It never went away, even when I'd stopped looking because I thought I'd found something else. Even when I thought that kind of Wicca just didn't exist anymore.

And here it was, apparently, as though from nothing. Oh shit. I had only checked on an alcohol-induced whim. There was *never* anything. Not in years. But here, a three-line post on a Pagan website that I hadn't bothered looking at in however many months: "Traditional Gardnerian Coven, North Carolina. We practice our tradition as it was passed to us by our Long Island elders. At this time, we are not currently accepting new students."

Like hell you're not.

I tossed back my drink like an action hero before he jumps off a cliff. Because this ad wasn't here the last time I was seeking. Last time, I'd emailed covens in Virginia, South Carolina, and Georgia. Last time, I'd driven four hours one way to circle with people who, though they were dear to me, knew plain well that I didn't belong. I'd just gotten out of a bad relationship. I'd just applied to graduate school. I'd just picked up and moved to a new city. I was ready to start my life over. This ad was here for me, I *knew* it.

Now I just needed to get them to let me in.

You Are Not Alone

There are a lot of Witches in the world.

If you're like most seekers, you probably feel pretty alone some-times. You look around you, at your friends, family, and coworkers, and marvel at the secret life you live. What would they think if they knew about you? Would they understand? Is there *anyone* who would understand? Maybe you live in a small town—the kind with a church at every intersection and where everyone knows everything about ev-eryone else (almost)—and you're sure you're the only magical person for miles. No Pagan shops, no meetups or moots, and no hope. Or maybe you live in a big city and your problem is on the other end of the spectrum: there are Witches and Pagans all over the place…just not the kind you're looking for. Whatever the case, most of us have the experience of feeling isolated and lonely. I don't know a single practi-tioner of any kind who hasn't spent time wishing for contact with oth-ers of like mind. Even if we're happy working alone, most of us reach out to others from time to time, whether online or in the flesh. We need to be able to share our experiences and ideas, to ask questions, and take comfort in companionship. When we can't do those things, it becomes very easy to feel like the only Witch in the world.

But here's the thing: you are *not* the only Witch in the world.

You're probably not even the only Witch in town (yes, even in your tiny church town). As alone as you may feel and as devoid of immediate resources as your surroundings may be on your aver-age day, it is extremely unlikely that there are no other practitioners nearby. Contemporary Pagans number in the hundreds of thousands in the United States alone (exact numbers vary widely depending on how we define "Pagan"), and many of those practice some kind of Witchcraft.[17] There are many more kinds of non-Pagan Witches, too,

---

17. James R. Lewis, "The Pagan Explosion: An Overview of Select Census and Sur-vey Data," in *The New Generation Witches: Teenage Witchcraft in Contemporary Culture*, ed. Hannah E. Johnston and Peg Aloi (Burlington: Ashgate Publishing Limited, 2007), 13–23.

so these numbers are probably low. Once you factor in neighboring towns and cities, it becomes harder and harder to insist that you're all alone in the world. You aren't.

You just haven't figured out where to look yet.

For many Witches—of any kind—the ultimate dream is to belong to a stable, working coven. Imagine: a tight-knit group of like-minded souls working together, advancing each other's practices, celebrating together, working powerful ritual and magic together. In traditional Wicca, belonging to a coven is the norm. An initiate may ultimately choose to work alone, or he may spend much of his time on his own (because of distance or the need to focus on other areas of life), but training occurs within a group setting. Even if that group is small—perhaps only a high priestess and one or two students—becoming a traditional Wiccan is a social process.

As a seeker, one of your first hurdles is locating and joining a coven within the tradition you want to practice. This can be an extremely daunting task. In this chapter, we'll talk about where to start, what to look for, and what to do when the going gets tough. However daunted you may feel, know that this is far from being an impossible task, and steady persistence pays off.

Before you even start seeking, you have to know what you're looking for. This sounds self-explanatory, but, as you've seen, there's a lot of variety within traditional Wicca. It usually isn't enough to say "I want to be Wiccan" or even "I want to be a traditional Wiccan." There are many Wiccan traditions operating today, and many different kinds of covens within each. Aside from considering which tradition appeals to you the most, you must also decide how much time you have to commit to training, how far you are willing to travel, and how well Wiccan training will fit into your life.

Know Thyself

As an exercise, consider the following questions. Get out a notebook and jot down some answers so that you can review your thoughts periodically and refocus. Some of your responses may change in time, and you can refer to these should you find yourself facing similar questions from a prospective coven (many of these I require inquiring seekers to answer before allowing them to attend an outer court circle):

1. What attracts you to traditional Wicca? Of all the kinds of Witchcraft in the world, why this one?

2. How do you feel about working skyclad? Having a working partner (and, most likely, having one of another sex and gender identity)?

3. How much time can you devote to a coven? Can you meet on weeknights? Weekends?

4. How far are you willing to travel? Can you do so reliably?

5. How does your partner or spouse feel about you being involved in a coven? How will they handle not having access to this part of your life? How do they feel about the prospect of you having to keep some of your experiences secret from them?

6. Are you comfortable with hierarchy, or would you prefer something more egalitarian?

7. Do you want to run your own coven someday? Can you do that in the tradition you're exploring?

8. What does your perfect coven look like? What kinds of things do they do? Are there a lot of people in it? How often do they meet?

9. Is your work life stable? Is your home life stable? Is now the right time to make a major change?

10. What are your short-term goals as a Witch? What are your long-term goals?

Answer these questions completely and honestly and you'll have a solid idea of what you should look for, what kinds of covens are worth approaching, and what obstacles you may encounter moving forward. If you work every weekend, you'll need to find a group that meets primarily during the week. If you're only available for meeting once a month, then you shouldn't join a coven that meets once a week. If you don't have your own car and can't travel outside of your own city, then you shouldn't be looking at covens fifty miles away. If your wife is unhappy with your decision to pursue Witchcraft, then you'll likely run into problems if you try to join a group that requires you to keep coven activities secret from her. If you're a man who aspires to run his own coven one day, then you shouldn't approach a tradition that passes authority exclusively through women.

Be as honest with yourself as possible. If you're not sure about something, admit and accept that. You're still exploring, after all! You can't possibly know exactly what to expect and what will work best for you at this point. This exercise just gives you a starting point—a way to cross some covens and traditions off your list immediately. It's not uncommon for seekers to meet with several groups before finding the best fit. It's also not uncommon for a seeker to spend time working with a coven—maybe even several months—and then come to the realization that it isn't a good fit. At the core of traditional Wiccan training and practice is the process of self-development—coming to know yourself and realizing your potential. You have to start exactly where you are. This means knowing your desires and goals as well as your fears and limitations. This is in your best interest and will ensure that you make the best match possible with a potential coven. Not only will you know what to look for, but you'll also know what questions to ask of coven leaders you may meet.

 FROM THE CIRCLE

When I left the Catholic Church and became Pagan, I was determined to never join another organized religion. But I missed the structure and the ritual. I missed the burning incense and people coming from all over to speak in unison to lend power to something greater than themselves. I compromised by going to open circles and ended up becoming friends with three other Witches. The rumor was that one of them was a traditional high priestess. Until this point, I had assumed that traditional Wiccans were an extinct branch of the Witchcraft evolutionary tree: where a lot of current Craft traditions came from, but no longer a living tradition. It was like I was talking to a living archaeopteryx (minus the bird-like shrieks). I asked a lot of questions, and she answered them when she could. Over the course of the year that I got to know her coven, I went from being mindfully skeptical and secretly jealous to timidly asking if I could attend outer court.

—*Acacia, outer court member*

Working Skyclad

Before we get too much farther, let's pause and consider one of traditional Wicca's most famously divisive characteristics, and one that many seekers initially struggle with: ritual nudity (or "skyclad" ritual). If you've been considering traditional Wicca for any length of time, you've probably already learned that it's typical for covens to perform the rites nude. Indeed, one of the most controversial things about early Wicca was its penchant for nudity in circle, and this is something that continues to raise some eyebrows. If the thought of taking your clothes off in front of a roomful of other people makes your stomach twist, know that you're not the only one. This is a hurdle that most seekers have to leap.

The thing is, skyclad ritual is *supposed* to be uncomfortable at first. It *should* feel out of the ordinary at first. Skyclad practice is part of the process of separating from the mundanity of your day-to-day. It's a magical trigger designed to put you in the mindset that allows for the extraordinary. It's also a sign of the profound trust that is required for successful work in a coven.

There are a number of reasons that various people cite for skyclad ritual. For some, it's a reference to a popular Wiccan text by Doreen Valiente (though many versions exist) called "The Charge of the Goddess," which includes the proclamation to be naked in your rites as a sign of freedom. For others, it's an equalizer. Stripped of our clothes and other symbols of status, who are we? It's also a symbol of our reverence for the physical. We revel in our bodies and our sexualities. Some practitioners also insist that clothing can inhibit the flow of magical energy (though I'd be more inclined to attribute that problem to practice).

Obviously, there are plenty of good reasons to practice clothed. When it's cold and rainy outside, you better believe I'm gonna be wearing something. Furthermore, when it's your body at stake, it's your call. No one should be trying to force you into something that you don't want to do. It's okay to choose to work robed or in street clothes if that's what you prefer. Just take that as an indicator that a particular tradition, coven, or coven leader isn't for you!

But if you're on the fence, it's worth challenging your discomfort. Ritual nudity in a safe environment can be enormously beneficial. Years of practicing skyclad with people I love and trust has taught me to value my own body in ways beyond the typically prescribed self-love routines. Just the act of seeing other naked bodies engaged in something positive—without concern for culturally prescribed standards of beauty—does something to alter our (usually unrealistic) expectations for ourselves. It makes us stronger Witches, because we develop the power to be at ease (more potent, even) in our own skins, regardless of what they look like or what they can do. Believe me, traditional Wiccans are just as fat, skinny, scarred, hairy, variously abled, and prone to body-image hang-ups as anyone. We just take it off *anyway*. It was a struggle for plenty of us. That confidence is something that *most* of us had to work up to. If you really think that the people in your potential coven are going to ridicule you, take this as an indicator that you're circling with the wrong people. In good ritual, the focus is on the work at hand. Not on your body.

The First Step

So now that you've got a sense of what you want, how do you actually start looking? Where should you look? Whom should you talk to?

Sometimes, being a seeker is a little like being a private investigator in a mystery novel. What you're looking for is rarely right in front of your face. You have to recognize clues, follow leads, ask the right questions, and be willing to take chances. Most importantly, you have to be willing to persevere when the trail goes cold. It can be a long, frustrating process. A lot of would-be Wiccans give up almost as soon as they begin simply because they don't have the patience to work past that initial difficulty of realizing that the perfect coven probably isn't operating next door.

Witchcraft is a broad and diverse practice, and as such it attracts a sometimes surprising variety of people. Often, when we struggle to find others in our communities, part of the problem is that we're making too many assumptions about what a Witch looks like and how they should choose to live. We tend to look for people who resemble ourselves, forgetting that other possibilities exist. More times than I can count in almost twenty years of Wiccan practice, I've been in the company of another Witch, listening to them complain about the absence of others, completely unaware that there was another Witch (and one who runs a coven, at that) in the room. In my professional life, I work to be inconspicuous. I tend to blend in with my fellow classroom teachers (I even have Wiccan students, and not a one knows their teacher is a Witch). Our personal lives—including our religious inclinations—aren't relevant to our work, so they rarely arise outside of the more intimate conversations we may have with our actual friends. There's no reason a coworker would suspect that I'm a Witch. I consciously don't *give* them a reason. That's a choice I've made, for the sake of maintaining my own privacy. And yet here I am. I don't stand out. You couldn't pick me out of a crowd. Nonetheless, I've built clear avenues for other Witches to find me, if they know how to look. And I'm not the only Witch leaving trails of breadcrumbs in the forest for seekers to find.

Making the Most of the Internet

Despite its prevalence—its everywhere-ness and our dependence on it—most of us are kind of bad at the internet. We can use it to do our jobs and keep tabs on our friends and families. We play games and catch up on the news and cruise social media sites for cat memes. Some of us consciously use it for research purposes, Googling "Wicca" or searching the hashtags on Tumblr or Wordpress for Witchcraft-related sites. What a lot of people don't realize, however, is that you can also use the internet to find covens, study groups, mentors, and friends. In the same way that you might reach out to find other *Game of Thrones* fans or other stay-at-home moms or other fountain pen collectors, you can find other people interested in whatever tradition of Witchcraft you can think of. There's a good chance that you've already done some exploring of the Pagan and Witch internet, and none of this is news. We *live* with the internet, after all. Even so, I'm often amazed by what people say they *can't* find, despite hours of ardent surfing, and I suspect that the issue lies with impatience rather than unfamiliarity. I lurk on a longstanding traditional Wiccan listserv where seekers may post inquiries, and I always chuckle to see my own city come up in conversation. Every time a beginner posts, "I can't find any Wiccans here!" I know that they either haven't looked or don't know *how* to look. So let's discuss some specific sites and strategies for making the most of your internet experience.

Most fundamentally, you'll need to refine your search skills. There's a balance to be struck between being too broad and being too narrow. Running a search for "Wicca" is going to turn up googobs of websites, most of which won't be what you're really looking for (and many of which will hurt more than they help). On the other hand, searching "Mohsian high priests in Salt Lake City" might turn up bupkus (although I don't actually know for sure...I haven't tried!). You have to know what you want, but you also have to be flexible. A good place to start is with "Wicca" and your state or city (or country, depending on how much geographic space that entails and what kind of travel is reasonable for you). That's how many seekers have found me. That's also how I found the coven that trained me. If that yields a lot of options, try narrowing things with "traditional Wicca" or even the specific tradition you're considering.

This kind of search may turn up many kinds of results. If you're lucky, you may find websites devoted to individual traditions or covens in your area. You may also find links to ads placed on websites like The Witches' Voice (www.witchvox.com) or small Pagan social media sites (www.wiccantogether.com). Many of these kinds of websites have been around for a long time (The Witches' Voice has been around since the nineties!), and sections of them are no longer being maintained regularly. Increasingly, people rely on larger social media sites like Facebook and don't even realize that specialized networking hubs exist. Even on these older sites, however, you may be able to turn up useful leads. Just because a group advertisement was placed a few years ago doesn't mean it's no good. It doesn't hurt to give it a try. This is especially true within older Wiccan traditions, whose elders may still rely on more dated contact media. A coven that's been running smoothly for twenty years may not feel the need to delete its tried-and-true Witchvox listing in favor of a Facebook page. You may even turn up a PO box address (I maintain one myself and have absolutely received seeker inquiries by mail). If you find a lead, try it!

In most cases, however, you won't turn up a whole website or a specific advertisement directed at local seekers. It's much more likely that you'll find social media profiles for Witches and Pagans living in that area. You may find blogs, too, which can be fantastic resources. If you find Instagram accounts, Tumblr pages, or similar personal internet spaces and the owner welcomes followers, add them! In following their regular posts—even if they're not directly about Witchcraft— you do two important things. First, you give yourself the opportunity to build a relationship with someone who could someday become a friend, a mentor, a covenmate, or a study partner. Second, you become connected to a larger network of people (other followers, linked blogs and other web pages, etc.), which means even more potential contacts, any one of whom may provide the key for moving forward in the future. Some of these people will specifically invite questions, comments, or other kinds of individualized input from people who find their accounts. Take advantage of this. On my own social media accounts, followers can contact me through comments and direct messaging. Over the years, I've built solid friendships this way.

Social media provides seekers with more opportunities for networking than ever before. Individual platforms come and go, but so many now exist that it's easy for anyone with a computer to reach out to others through many mediums. You can go to YouTube or Vimeo and watch videos by thousands of other Witches and Pagans of all kinds (both professional, informational videos and unpolished, personal clips from practitioners just sharing their lives using home recorders). You can explore Witch-related hashtags on Instagram, Tumblr, and Twitter to find personal pictures, links, and blog posts. And you can search sites like Facebook, Meetup, and even old standbys like Yahoo! Groups for groups and listservs that provide networking opportunities for seekers. Social media changes constantly, and platforms certainly have a shelf life. By the time you read this, there may be a half dozen new places to build your online home. Take advantage of what's available! Many Witches create accounts specifically for their Witchcraft and use them to reach out to others, collect information, and share their experiences. The more of these you explore, the more likely you are to find people close to home (or people who *know* people close to home). Every new contact represents possibility.

Beyond just searching for resources in your own area, look for those with broader reach. There are websites out there that cater to particular traditions, and some of these maintain pages designed to help seekers find covens. Search the names of specific traditions, favorite authors, or famous practitioners (living and dead). These broader searches will reveal more resources than what you're likely to find when you add your region or city. Follow all leads, no matter how small. Can you find a blog written by someone who works within the tradition you're pursuing? They may be able to point you to a local group that isn't vocal online. Contact them. Can you find other seekers to the same tradition you're studying? Ask them about their experiences. Reach out to other people, even if it seems far-fetched. Worst-case scenario is usually that you just don't get a response.

Casting the Net

Seeking isn't easy. Maybe you will be lucky enough to find covens and other kinds of groups and open events relatively nearby. Maybe when you ran your first internet search for "traditional Wiccan coven near me," you were blessed to find two coven listings, a big meetup group for all local Pagans, and a dozen blogs maintained by local Witches, just writing about their lives and posting pictures of their friends, families, and homes. Maybe you found the address of a local shop that caters to Pagans and occultists. Lucky you!

It's more likely, however, that you didn't find quite that much. In fact, maybe you found none of it. Like I said, seeking isn't easy, and this first part is sometimes the hardest. For some people, it's a lot harder than for others. But now isn't the time to give up in despair. Just because that first, simplest internet search didn't turn anything up doesn't mean that you're the only Witch in town. It just means that they aren't advertising. At least, they aren't advertising via the most popular channels. It's time to cast a wider net.

Many different kinds of people practice Witchcraft, it's true. Making too many assumptions can inhibit our seeking. But it's also true that certain kinds of people seem to be more likely to feel drawn to practice the Craft, study magic, and worship the old gods (or abandon all talk of gods entirely, seeking their power elsewhere, as many Witches do). Witchcraft—no matter what kind of Witchcraft we're talking about—

exists on the margins. Whether or not we individually think it's right and fair—if we believe Wicca deserves the same kind of recognition as any other respectable religion, or if we feel that Witchcraft is *necessarily* an art that belongs only to the marginalized—the Craft resists the mainstream. Secret by nature and harboring ideas that often challenge conventional society, Witchcraft tends to attract people who are at least somewhat unconventional *already*. To find other Witches, it is often useful to traverse other spaces that draw these personalities. Certain Witchcraft communities overlap with other "alternative" or "fringe" movements, subcultures, and interest groups. These terms are often used dismissively, in contrast to the "mainstream," which is itself a kind of myth that fails to account for the individual complexity of people (in this age, the "alternative" may be the majority, and what appears "mainstream" may be only a veneer). Nonetheless, here we can use this kind of categorization to positive ends.

Over the decades, Wiccan Witchcraft, collectively, has come to emphasize certain concerns, which give it some distinction (whether or not any of these may be central to individual covens or practitioners). Speaking broadly, these are nature and the environment, sexuality and gender, health and personal development, and the practice of magic. Various components of Wicca—the celebration of seasonal sabbats, skyclad ritual, a gendered pair of deities, the practice of spellcraft, a generally open attitude toward sex and sexuality, and others—naturally extend into other fields. Consequently, it is often easier to find other Wiccans (as well as other kinds of Witches and Pagans) amongst communities that share these interests and concerns. You may have difficulty finding a local store specifically serving Witches, but is there one specializing in health and holistic healing? Is there a gem and mineral store? A feminist bookshop? Maybe there's no Pagan meetup, but is there one for environmentalists and other outdoor lovers? People with these interests may be more likely to also have an interest in Witchcraft or related practices. Be creative here. The wider the net you cast, the more leads you are likely to find. Some connections are clearer than others. For example, I once lived in a city that didn't have a Pagan meetup (sometimes called a moot), but it did have one for tarot readers. Whether or not I was passionate about tarot (and I wasn't, at first), I suspected that at least some members would probably also be Pagans or Witches, and may be able to point me to other communities. I was right. There were several people who, I found out in time as I got to know them, were solitary practitioners or part of small, private covens with no internet presence. I could have Googled from dawn to dusk and I never would have found them.

Other communities may also have connections, though they are less obvious. Queer, feminist, and kink communities often attract Witches and Pagans, as all of these groups tend to share "progressive" or "alternative" attitudes toward sex, sexuality, and gender. You may also find contacts and other resources within communities interested in folklore, history (particularly in eras somehow pertaining to Witchcraft or Pagan religion), mythology, and fantasy. Groups like the Society for Creative Anachronism (SCA) are famous for harboring Pagans and occultists, thanks to a shared interest in European history. You'll find a disproportionately large number of Pagans in historical European martial arts (HEMA) groups, for similar reasons. Gamer and fandom communities are also good places to find others, particularly those bent toward fantasy, magic, and horror.

Do not fall into the trap of assuming that just because you can't find groups, meetups, or shops that are explicitly Wiccan that you must be alone. Witches are complex people with varied interests, but some patterns are discernible. If "Wicca" turns up nothing in your online searching, expand it to "Witchcraft," "Pagan," "occult," or "New Age." Consider which of your other interests might appeal to fellow Witches. In exploring, you may even discover new interests. Creativity and persistence are key.

Regardless how fruitful your local search for fellow Witches, it's very likely that at some point you'll have to move beyond your familiar surroundings and venture into unexplored territory. This will be especially true if the parameters you've set for your ideal coven are somewhat narrow. You may be determined to become an initiate of Alexandrian Wicca, but there may simply be no Alexandrian covens in your city. If this is the case, you'll have to seek further afield. Even if there were twelve Alexandrian covens in your immediate area, it would still be worthwhile to explore the other options that may be available to you. Fifty miles away, you may find a coven with a more compatible high priestess or a better group dynamic. Even happily co-vened Witches benefit from meeting other Witches and Pagans from other traditions or other lines within their own traditions. You can use the same strategies for finding others that you used locally, with some additional possibilities.

 FROM THE CIRCLE

The most challenging thing was finding a group that was the right fit for me. I believe too many seekers are in a hurry and just want to get going. I was no exception to this. Do your best to be patient. Explore! Look everywhere until you find what is right. Understand, too, that traditional Wicca may not be right for you. Be honest. Don't know what you don't know. You can't bullshit experienced Witches—they'll see through you if you pretend you're more knowledgeable than you really are. If you don't know something, just say so!

—*Liam, third degree high priest*

Attending Festivals and Open Events

The Pagan festival movement has been going strong for decades. Born in the same spirit as the music and consciousness-raising festivals popular in the era of the American counterculture, Pagan festivals are opportunities for practitioners of myriad traditions to come together to celebrate, learn, teach, and enjoy their own space, apart from the mundane. There are many festivals all over the United States and in many parts of Europe and Canada. Some are impromptu weekend events put on by single Pagan groups, open to the community. Others are annual events that last for whole weeks and draw in hundreds (or even thousands) from other regions. Festivals often offer a program of workshops, author talks and book signings, musical performances, and plenty of ritual. Organizers may bring in Pagan presenters, or offer classes taught by local experts. There may be fireside drumming and dancing, outdoor activities like hiking and camping, and plenty of time to socialize with different kinds of practitioners. These types of events are fantastic opportunities to network. At larger festivals, many traditions will be represented, and you need only ask an organizer to point you in the right direction. You never know who you could meet!

Festivals usually involve travel and require taking time away from work. There are also admission costs, plus the expense of food and lodging (whether that means hotel fees or camping supplies). For most of us, careful planning and saving throughout the year are critical. But if you're hungry to meet others and find a place in a wider community, the cost may be well worth it. I have been to several different festivals over the years, but one in particular—Free Spirit Gathering in Maryland—has become my summer home. Whatever else is going on in my life, I do everything in my power to be there every year to enjoy my festival family. Even after becoming a member of a traditional coven with established practices, the experiences I've had at Free Spirit have continued to influence my Witchcraft and my relationships with the gods. I continue to learn and grow every summer, even though (actually, because) we come from different paths. That's the real benefit of festival.

If one of these larger events sounds appealing, be aware that they offer different amenities and have different rules. Plan accordingly. Do you mind being in a tent for a week, or would you prefer something indoors, where you can purchase a hotel room? Some events are outdoors but on campgrounds with furnished cabins and indoor plumbing. Will you have to bring your own food for each day, or is there a meal plan available for an additional fee? Are workshops free, or do some have a speaker or supply cost? How do you feel about clothing-optional events? Many outdoor festivals allow nudity. This usually does not include the possibility of public sex acts, but there are certainly adult-only festivals where this may be permitted. Are you looking for an event where you can include your children? Some festivals have children's programming or childcare. Others may allow children but not provide for any of their specific needs, leaving it to parents to find ways to entertain and educate. Be aware, too, that many festivals allow nudity but also have children in attendance. This may influence your decision to bring your own kids. Some events cater to specific Pagan groups or traditions, and others are more inclusive. Depending on how far you are willing to travel and how much funding you have available, you have much to consider. It's also worthwhile to see if an individual festival offers a work option, "scholarship," or other type of assistance for attendees who may not be able to pay the full cost. Many do!

Most of the largest festivals maintain websites that will come up with relatively simple internet searches, along with useful festival guides (try searching "Pagan festivals" and adding your region).[18] You can also visit the websites of your favorite Witch writers, musicians, internet personalities, and speakers to see if they'll be appearing at any events nearby. Don't forget to ask the people in your network what events they love! You may have to travel, but you could also be lucky enough to find something fun right under your nose.

If a long festival is out of the question for now (or even if it's not), there are many other kinds of open Pagan events that may be available to you. In the United States, Pagan Pride Day events are becomingly increasingly common and popular, particularly near larger cities. Usually, Pagan Pride Day occurs at some point in the fall and doesn't last beyond a weekend. These are public, free events that are designed to spread awareness of the growing influence of Pagan religions and to

---

18. Wiccan author Jason Mankey publishes an extensive list of summer festivals every year on his blog, which you can visit at www.patheos.com/blogs/panmankey.

build community amongst Pagans and their neighbors. Often, donations are collected for local charities. There are vendors selling Pagan goods, teachers offering workshops, and often special guest speakers and performers. Your own town may not have a Pagan Pride Day (though you could start one!), but it's very possible that a neighboring city does. Make a road trip, if you can, and spend the day making friends and learning from others.

You may also be able to find meetups, Pagan night out events, open rituals, and workshops at Pagan stores. Many Unitarian Universalist churches offer Pagan events or even have an organized CUUPS group (Covenant of Unitarian Universalist Pagans). Meeting other Pagans may very well mean going to church on Sunday morning! Even if you can only commit to attending any of these things once, they are worth seeking out. There are many Witches who frequent these kinds of events specifically to find like-minds to establish private groups and covens. It hardly matters whether or not the ritual or class is directly relevant to your specific practice or even if it's particularly good. The real point is to make contacts. You may not be interested in a class on ancestor offerings in Druid traditions or in a public ritual for the new moon, but *go anyway*. It's very likely that there will be at least one other person in attendance who is *also* only scouting for friends. I assembled my first ritual group through relationships that I built over dozens of open events, many of which were not even remotely resembling my proverbial cup of tea. Don't miss the opportunity to participate in your wider community, even if it's an approximation. Just because there's no one putting together public events that appeal exactly to you doesn't mean that there aren't others out there who practice (or aspire to practice) as you do. A little boredom or frustration is a fair price to pay for finding your tribe. Go. And then mind your mouth and don't be a snob; you never know who's listening.

No matter where you end up looking and no matter what strategies you use to find others, it's going to take time and a lot of patience. If you are lucky, you may find a coven within your desired tradition near to you and accepting new students. But it's more likely that you will have to build a network, ask around, go to events, follow internet leads, and venture out into a wider community. You will find your way forward taking baby steps, not giant leaps.

Seeking is a process. Before initiation, before training even begins, there is this first test. Do you have the patience to wait? Are you diligent enough to persist in the face of discouragement? Are you creative enough to recognize opportunity beyond your original vision? Are you brave enough to reach out? For many, this first step is the most challenging. It's a rare person who stumbles into the perfect coven with minimal effort. Sometimes, that lack of an initial struggle makes such a person overly soft, vulnerable in future trials of patience and commitment. We tend to value those things that we have to work and wait for over those that simply fall in our lap. So when you're feeling frustrated, remind yourself that this is part of the process, not some cosmic indication that this path isn't for you. Keep practicing your own Craft. When you're feeling lonely, practice Witchcraft. When you're unsure of where to look next, or you're reeling from a false start, practice Witchcraft. Finding home with the right coven can take years. Don't wait until then to figure out who you are as a Witch. All of that effort can only serve you and ultimately push you to where you should be. Practice. Learn. Try. Be brave.

CHAPTER 8

BECOMING A STUDENT

There is an adage that floats around magical communities. You've probably heard it before. It goes like this: when the student is ready, the teacher appears.

This is bullshit.

Rather, the underlying implication that the student need only sit around waiting is bullshit.

This little aphorism is popularly attributed to the Buddha, but its origins are quite a bit murkier than that. Far from being the piece of Eastern wisdom transcending the ages that much of the internet thinks it is, this famous bit of occult lore was popularized in the late nineteenth century by the Theosophical Society. Founded in the United States in 1875 by Helena Blavatsky and Henry Steel Olcott (amongst others), the Theosophical Society was interested in the pursuit of universal wisdom through the study of various occult systems, as well as other branches of religion, philosophy, and science. The idea was to further the spiritual evolution of the human race through the propagation of the teachings of the "ascended masters" (various great religious leaders and teachers, as well as spiritual beings who spoke directly to the society's leaders). Though there have been significant changes since its formation, the Theosophical Society exists today, and it has done much to expose white occultists to other ideas and traditions. Unfortunately, this has also contributed to the fetishizing of nonwhite cultures, wherein we make assumptions about a group's inherent value based on our romanticized, obscured view of them. The same mode of thinking that justifies the myth of the "noble savage" in the Americas gives us the "wise Eastern master" in Asia.[19]

When we uncritically repeat such pieces of mystical wisdom, especially shortsighted ones like the above, we do ourselves a serious disservice. If we're generous, we could look at such a statement about the relationship between occult students and teachers and observe that the "ready" student is aware that everyone around him has lessons to teach. In growing, the whole world becomes his teacher. There's certainly some merit to this. At worst, however, we may be tempted to use this as permission to sit around waiting, simply trusting that eventually the right mentor or coven leader will stumble along and recognize us as one of their own. We give things up to "fate" or "the universe" and in turn absolve ourselves of any responsibility for achieving our own ends. While there are certainly people in the world with such lucky stories, this is not a bet you want to make. It is one thing to be patient (and this remains ever a virtue) but quite another to be lazy.

As a coven leader and high priestess with the authority to bring new practitioners into my tradition, I don't comb New Age bookstores or internet forums looking for people to initiate. I've never stalked someone from afar, ultimately approaching them from the shadows to say, "Hey, you seem like you're ready to move forward. Here's my phone number and the address of my covenstead. Why don't you come to circle this weekend?"

That's not going to happen. This is not a tower, and you are not a princess. There's no one coming to rescue you. Slay your own dragon.

I'm *already* a Wiccan initiate. My seeker days are long over, and I'm not going to do anyone else's work for them. I'm not going to

---

19. For more on this phenomenon, consider Jane Naomi Iwamura's *Virtual Orientalism: Asian Religions and American Popular Culture* (New York: Oxford University, 2011).

hunt you down, pick you up off the internet, or respond to your public pleas for a teacher. It's your task to reach out to *me*, not the other way around.

So how exactly do you do that? Once you've found a coven or a potential mentor, how do you actually reach out to them? How do you convince a secretive Witch group to let you through those shrouded doors and into the circle?

The Fyne Arte of Introductions

So by now, you've been seeking for a while. You've scoured the internet, you've followed local leads, you've attended open Pagan events, and you've continued reading whatever you can get your hands on. You've got your sights set on a particular tradition or even a particular coven. It's time to make your move.

This is a lot less cloak-and-dagger than many people suppose. There's no coded language or secret riddle. You don't have to stand silently on anyone's doorstep or be rejected three times before being allowed in.[20] You don't need a secret handshake. Instead, you need something quite a bit rarer and more valuable: good manners.

In the early days of Wicca, seekers often contacted covens through the postal system. Covens and seekers alike posted their addresses in various occult and magically inclined periodicals, inviting inquiries from like minds. Letters might be exchanged several times before those involved met face to face. Sometimes, this meant one party traveled a considerable way to receive training (remember the Bucklands, who crossed an ocean in pursuit of Gardnerian Wicca). Other times, information was passed entirely through the post, allowing for the building of tradition across distance, as was the case for many of those influenced by Robert Cochrane and Joe Wilson. In any case, letter

---

20. Although, the tradition of being denied admission three times does have a precedent in some occult fraternities, so it's not *impossible* that you'll run into it amongst Witches.

writing played a critical role in the development and spread of many kinds of contemporary Witchcraft.

Nowadays, we don't send many letters, but we nonetheless rely on written language. We send emails, we post to online forums and social media sites, and we send text messages. You don't need to be a brilliant writer. It's much more important that you be polite and direct. Your task is to put your best foot forward, express your interest, and set yourself apart from other seekers who may have reached out recently. Depending on how prominent and outspoken the coven, its leaders may receive several inquiries a month. Even the largest coven can't take every seeker who knocks on the door. We have to make choices, and, like an employer evaluating a resume, we do so based on potentially tiny details.

Reaching out to a teacher or a coven (or just someone you believe can direct you to one) requires that you be polite and express yourself clearly and respectfully. You've already spent a good deal of time considering your goals, your needs, and your past experiences. Now you have to honestly convey those things to someone else who, at least theoretically, has the power to help you get to where you want to be. What's critical to understand is this: you are not entitled to Wiccan training. That teacher or coven leader owes you *nothing*. There's nothing that requires them to even respond to you, let alone invite you to attend an outer court ritual. A high priestess or high priest of traditional Wicca is charged with the protection of their coven and the preservation of their Craft. That doesn't entail taking in every seeker who finds their email address and sends unsolicited questions. A lot of time and work go into maintaining a coven, and on top of that we may have mundane jobs, family obligations, and all the responsibilities that go along with being adults in the world. Most simply don't have time or energy to devote special attention to anyone and everyone who asks for it. That initial correspondence makes or breaks you, so let's look at the finer points of making a good impression and improving your odds of receiving consideration.

Let me go ahead and give you another glimpse into my own life as a coven leader so that you'll have a better idea of how things look from the other side:

As the high priestess of one of the few traditional Wiccan covens in my state, and as a public Witch with an active internet presence, I receive inquiries from seekers every week. This number easily doubles at Halloween and every time a new movie or television show about Witches or magic finds its way into mainstream circulation. Most of these messages still arrive via my coven profile at the Witches' Voice (www.witchvox.com), although every now and then someone will contact me through my personal website or blog. Although I read every single one, I respond to almost none of them. Usually, they go immediately into the trash bin.

Why? Am I just heartless? Deaf to the pleas of the spiritually wayward? Isn't it my religious duty and moral imperative to assist those who stumble to my virtual doorstep?

Nope.

I don't take any pleasure in the struggle of others. Those of you out there looking for your Craft family, I feel you. Believe me. That's why I'm writing to you now! I'm not heartless. What I *am* is experienced enough to evaluate inquiries with relative accuracy based on the tone and content of the message. Those that get ignored usually commit one of two sizable faux pas: either they contain only superficial questions and reveal no information about the seeker, or they make demands and reflect a gross sense of entitlement.

I am not a search engine or the Wiccan version of customer service. Still, some people insist on treating me like their personal answer mill. This is particularly irritating for coven leaders who maintain websites or who belong to traditions where information is readily available (even Wikipedia has some pretty extensive pages on a number of Wiccan traditions). Don't be one of those people. Before you contact a potential coven, do your homework. Research the tradition. Read any available books about the tradition. Do an internet search on the coven itself. Serious seekers put in the effort of learning absolutely as much as they can before they make contact, so there's no need to ask obvious questions. You wouldn't show up to a job interview, declare that you desperately want to work for the company in question, and then immediately ask what it *does*. Your application would go straight to the bottom of the pile. Likewise, don't approach a coven without knowing whatever you can about their tradition. Being a novice is perfectly acceptable—you can't know everything!—but demonstrate that you've at least done the legwork. Don't let anyone mistake you for lazy!

Even more frustrating than receiving messages like, "I want to be in your coven. What's a Gardnerian?" are those who say things like "I want to be in your coven. Tell me how to become a Gardnerian." See the difference? The first is lazy. The second is lazy *and* entitled. If I answered every single message like this that shows up in my inbox, I wouldn't have much energy left for the good ones. On a good day, a thoughtless question might receive an answer, but a demand never will. As a seeker, you are the one approaching the coven. You are the one asking for attention. You are the one making the appeals. From their perspective, Wicca doesn't need you and Wicca isn't asking for you. Traditional coven leaders may make themselves available, trusting that sincere, worthy seekers will find them. What they won't do is play salesperson with a stranger on the internet. A seeker who begins by making demands will probably fare poorly when confronted by secrecy, hierarchy, and the requirement for patience. A seeker who begins by demonstrating a refusal to conduct independent inquiry or to pursue all available opportunities to learn is unlikely to succeed in an environment that requires independence and perseverance. Thus, I choose to ignore such messages out of my own desire to minimize wasted time, both mine and theirs. It's not heartlessness; it's mercy.

Okay, that's enough scary talk about what *not* to do. Let's get to some of the things that you *should* include in your opening. And guess what? If you spent some time thinking about the questions in chapter 7, getting to know yourself and pinpointing your own Craft needs, you've already done most of the work! A seeker who's already got a handle on his own needs, goals, and limitations is miles ahead of one who hasn't considered these things at all. Even if you feel overwhelmed, underprepared, or woefully ignorant about the tradition you're pursuing—driven by a sense of calling alone—your best strategy is to cultivate self-awareness. This is what you need to convey to a potential high priestess or high priest.

It's helpful to imagine that you're writing a cover letter to a potential employer (well, if that employer were a Witch). Begin by introducing yourself and sharing some of the more significant points of who you are. You're not just some random person with poorly conceived fantasies about learning Witchcraft; you've got unique experiences and a personality that sets you apart! You've spent a lot of time thinking about who you are and what your goals are. Those are the kinds of things you need to address in an opening letter. Get the mundane stuff out of the way (your name, your age, your occupation, your relative proximity to the coven, and that sort of thing), and then explain why you're interested in training. The high priest or high priestess who's going to read your message already knows that you want to know more about Wicca. They already know you're interested in joining a coven. They get these kinds of inquiries regularly. What they don't know is who you are and why you're approaching them as opposed to someone else.

As a coven leader considering a seeker, these are some of the things I want to know when someone first reaches out to me:

1. Why do you want to be initiated into *my* tradition? There are a lot of different kinds of Witchcraft and many other kinds of Wicca, after all. What do you think is so special about mine?

2. Have you been practicing Witchcraft on your own? Do you have experience in other kinds of groups?

3. What do you think I can offer you? What do you think you're going to learn with my coven? What do you have to offer us?

4. Why is now a good time for you to begin training with a coven? What does the rest of your life look like that there's room to commit to traditional training?

5. What are your strengths? What do you think you'll struggle with?

That's a lot of information, I know! But this is heavy stuff. You're asking for something significant, and you need to make it clear that you're serious from the get-go. If you can touch on most of these points in your opening inquiry, you will immediately set yourself apart as someone special. You don't have to use five-dollar words or impress anyone with your mastery of formal English syntax. You also don't have to write an autobiography. Traditional Wicca isn't only for the overly literate. You just have to be honest, thoughtful, and direct. The most important thing in your letter is *you*. Who are you? Why are you pursuing traditional Wicca? What are you bringing to the table? Don't get bogged down asking too many questions to start; you'll have that opportunity once the conversation begins. For now, focus on introducing yourself and explaining what you want and why you want it. Why do you *deserve* the trust that comes with being brought into a tradition? Seekers who can clearly demonstrate the effort they've already put into this process stand the best chance of being offered a place in a coven.

FROM THE CIRCLE

It's imperative that you have a deep trust for any high priestess or high priest that you decide to connect with. Your high priestess and high priest will plan rituals, determine when and if you are ready for elevation, be your spiritual guide, and so much more. If you don't feel that trust, you may need to seek out a different coven or look at other options. Ideally, a good traditional Wicca candidate needs to have some amount of self-awareness already developed. Working in a coven naked with a dozen other people can bring up all sorts of triggers. If you aren't equipped to have conversations about what is coming up for you, you may not be ready. You can't wait for a coven to fulfill all your spiritual development. Having a daily practice, making your personal spiritual work a priority, and working on your own practice are important and will make coven work and ritual so much more rewarding.

—*Phoenix LeFae, Wiccan priestess and Reclaiming Witch*

Vetting

There's a good chance that, after you've sent that initial email, direct message, or letter, you'll spend the next few days stressing about a reply. When it finally comes—especially if this is your first time reaching out—it's hard not to feel a little giddy. It's exciting stuff!

The next step is called vetting, in which a coven leader will try her best to decide whether or not to give you the opportunity to work with her coven. There isn't a formula here—you'll simply engage in conversation and try to get a feel for each other. This may happen through email, telephone, direct messaging on a social media site, or a digital hangout, and usually culminates in a face-to-face meeting.

Some coven leaders actually develop stock questionnaires to send to potential initiates, just like the kind you might have to fill out for a potential employer. These can really vary. Some questions are purely practical, covering your age, marital status, living situation, and similar bits of mundanity. Others get right down into your experience of the Craft, asking probing questions about what you've read, how you think about the gods, and what your personal practice looks like. I've met high priestesses who pride themselves on the extensiveness of the surveys they require seekers to complete—sometimes several pages worth of information. Theoretically, these questions allow a potential teacher to evaluate a student's fit with minimal investment on the coven's part. A sincere seeker will be patient enough to answer the questions completely and honestly, and then the coven can decide based on whatever criteria it chooses.

Personally, I prefer to ask questions prompted by the content of the seeker's initial inquiry, rather than immediately relying on something generic. If a seeker has engaged me effectively, I will genuinely want to know more about them and appropriate questions will spring to mind without prompting. When you're curious about someone, asking more about them comes naturally. If they don't come up on their own over the course of conversation, I will ask a handful of stock questions. Usually, this includes things like "How does your significant other feel about your desire to be Wiccan?" and "Can you reliably attend circles?" These are common sticking points for seekers, and I ask purely for the sake of practicality. Someone may be brilliant and fascinating, but if they can't physically get to our covenstead or if they have emotional hang-ups about doing so, then there's little point in moving forward. My favorite question to ask seekers is "What does your ideal coven look like?" This tells me a lot about them quickly and about their potential fit for my coven. I'm either offering what they want or I'm not.

If you do receive some kind of questionnaire, it's likely that most of the information required will be relatively noninvasive, but pay attention. Often, the kinds of questions that a coven leader asks will be very telling. Coven leaders usually learn to ask specific questions of seekers in light of direct experience—good or bad—and these may reveal their values, prejudices, preferences, and personal hang-ups. It's always your right to refrain from sharing something, to ask to discuss something sensitive another time (like when you meet in person), or to respond with your own questions. In fact, you *should* respond with your own questions. Remember, they're not the only ones who get to do the deciding! You need to take this opportunity to figure out if this coven is a match for you, too.

Most initial conversations with seekers begin just like any other first encounter. You'll exchange messages or emails, getting to know each other and determining if there's cause to meet in person. If you both decide to move forward, it's likely that you'll begin by meeting in a public place. My own high priestess still jokes that one of our local fast food chains must surely be enchanted by now, given how many Wiccan priests and priestesses began their coven journeys in one of those hallowed vinyl booths. Wherever you meet, be sure to come prepared with good manners and thoughtful questions. Relax, be yourself, be honest, and just try to get a feel for the people you're meeting. It's really not all that different from going on a first date! You want to do what you can to make a good impression, but not in such a way that you obscure who you really are for the sake of someone who isn't right for you.

If all goes well, the next step is usually an invitation to participate in some kind of coven or outer court activity. This may be purely social—a chance to mingle with others in the group in a more private environment—or it may entail participation in a ritual. Some coven leaders maintain social relationships with potential students for lengthy periods of time before inviting them to the covenstead. Don't be discouraged if you feel as though you're being held at arm's length. This is common. Take what opportunity you can to interact with members of the group and focus on building relationships, whether or not they center upon magical practice. When you are given the opportunity to come to a circle, a meal at the covenstead, or another private group engagement, be prompt, bring a small contribution (a bottle of wine, a side dish, flowers for the host, or some such token), and be sure you know what is expected of you! Is there some ritual tool or special clothing item you'll be asked to bring or wear? Is there a book you should have read? It's always useful to carry a notebook of some sort, too, so you can jot down questions or thoughts as you have them, as well as remember whatever important information you may need for next time (and you can add all of this to your personal journal or Book of Shadows later).

 FROM THE CIRCLE

We don't have an outer court. We have two covens, an eclectic one and a Gardnerian one. Both exist as separate entities in our minds even though both meet in our house and share some Witches. Having two covens has worked out really well for us, and we find it preferable to the traditional outer court. There are a lot of really great Witches out there who have no desire to become initiates and would probably be poorly suited to it. Having an eclectic coven allows us to continue to work with those people and learn from them.

Outer courts are a lot like waiting rooms. Becoming a part of one leads to the expectation that you'll eventually be moving on to something else, in this case initiation. Not having an outer court removes that expectation from the people we circle with, which can distract from the work we do. Today's Pagan world is a huge and thriving thing, and there are lots of different avenues that can be used to figure out if someone would make a good initiate. We don't think outer court is the only barometer of that. Many traditions outside of British traditional Wicca prepare Witches for initiation.

—*Ari Mankey and Jason Mankey, coven leaders in California*

Each coven has its own process. You may be formally offered membership in an outer court, or you may continue to interact and circle with coven members over an extended period, learning as you go. Sometimes, you must ask directly to be considered for initiation— it won't simply be extended to you. We'll talk more about how training actually works in the next chapter. Before we move on, let's look at what can happen when things go wrong.

Recognizing Red Flags

In this chapter and the last, we discussed the process of locating and then joining a coven. I've walked you through the often daunting task of meeting potential mentors and asking for training. As you've seen by now, every coven and every teacher has slightly different procedures for bringing in newcomers, vetting seekers, and ultimately passing their tradition on to a new generation of Witches. You may encounter quite a lot of variety as you explore, which is why it's important to generally know what you want in a coven. But just as important as knowing what you want is having a sense of what you *don't* want. Further, it's important to be able to recognize downright dysfunction.

Maybe you've already heard horror stories about what can happen to hapless seekers who stumble into unscrupulous teachers and covens. Maybe that's the thing that's gotten in the way of your seeking up to this point. A lot of Witches who may otherwise be interested in coven work never pursue it because they're concerned about all the things that can go wrong when a group gets involved, especially given how personal Craft practice is. It's not untrue that Pagan, Witch, and other occult communities sometimes act as a refuge for the unsavory, the unstable, or simply the melodramatic. Witchcraft tends to attract the marginalized. Given that so many of us have experienced the pain of exclusion, there is often a deep-seated reluctance to exclude others. You'll encounter all types of people in our communities. Most of the time, this is one of our greatest strengths, and very few people are genuinely out to take advantage of you, prey upon you, or otherwise do you harm. It's much more likely that you'll encounter self-appointed adepts and Witch queens out to collect peons without possessing the credentials or experience to back up their claims. You'll also probably meet people who seek validation though collecting titles, students, or local notoriety. You'll find people who will brag about their unsurpassed magical knowledge, namedrop their prestigious connections, and even discourage you in the pursuit of your own path because it makes them feel superior. Those kinds of people are certainly out there, and they're usually best handled with laughter. Never take their words personally.

Finally, you'll also encounter people who are genuinely struggling with difficult personal issues, working to build a home in a community known for its acceptance. Hey, plenty of us have been there, myself included, so handle such folks with compassion. Even the people who come off as jerks are usually just doing the best they can to deal with all the challenges that life can throw. Overwhelmingly, you will meet good, sincere people who mean well. But as a seeker, it's not a great idea to make other people's problems—whether they're emotional, financial, romantic, or professional—your problems. Further, though they're rare, there are absolutely predatory people in traditional Wiccan communities, just as there are in every community, and it's important to keep an eye out for red flags. Here are a few potential signs that you should steer clear of a particular teacher or coven:

They refuse to meet you in public.

It's one thing to be private. A certain degree of secrecy just goes along with being a Witch, but be wary of someone who flat-out refuses to have your first meeting in a public place. After a round of emails and phone calls, it's very common to meet up with potential covenmates at coffee shops or restaurants, or even local Pagan events. This allows both parties to size each other up without the fear of being cornered in a secluded place. In the same way that you wouldn't meet a blind date off of the internet at their unlisted address (this is so obviously the beginning to some horror movie somewhere), it's not a great idea to go immediately to a stranger's home or covenstead. Use your head and be safe. If there are legitimate reasons why a potential high priestess or high priest *can't* meet you in public (for example, illness that renders them homebound), it is fair to ask if you can bring a friend. Put your safety first.

They immediately offer you initiation.

By now, it should be clear to you how significant rites of initiation are to traditional Wiccans. The decision to bring someone new into the coven is a heavy one that takes forethought, planning, and a lot of trust. It's not something that's ever done lightly. Nonetheless, it's not impossible that you'll encounter people anxious to initiate or dedicate you right away. There are plenty of people online advertising for coven members ("coven seeking priestesses" or "high priest looking to train students for powerful Witchcraft" and similar ridiculousness). Traditional Wiccans rarely advertise in this manner, if ever, especially nowadays. Often, such covens aren't covens at all, but individuals looking to start them. The people behind the screen (or looking you in the eye at a public event) may be entirely benign and well-meaning, but it is very likely that they are, at least, only seekers themselves. Be cautious with someone who tries to become too intimate too quickly.

The conversation quickly turns to money and training fees.

While there are some kinds of Witchcraft in which adepts charge their students fees, traditional Wicca isn't one of them. Training and initiation never entail financial profit for coven leaders. There are several reasons for this, both magical and practical. Let's revisit our fictional high priestess, Glinda, to illustrate some of the problems around accepting money for Wiccan initiation:

Glinda is a hard worker. Aside from running her coven and serving as an elder in Flying Cat Wicca, she works a full-time job, takes care of her two children, and manages a household. She's a busy woman. For the last little while, she's been running both an outer court and an inner court, and this has her pretty much worn ragged. She's also put a lot of hard work and many years' worth of training to get where she is today. After a lot of thought, she decides that she's going to start charging her Craft students for their training. She charges for her time and energy most everywhere else in her life, after all. People pay her for tarot readings, for the candles she makes, and for the labor she does at her mundane job. Likewise, she pays others for their own services. Her teaching and her Witchcraft are skills, like any other, and surely she deserves to be compensated. It's only fair.

For a while, this seems to work out okay, and she comes to depend on this as a component of her regular income. And people are certainly willing to pay! She's an experienced Witch and a skilled teacher. Her life becomes more manageable. But something is happening in her coven, and the shift is so gradual that some don't even notice it. Glinda has lost a worthy student because he wasn't able to pay the monthly fee. She's also taken on a slightly less-than-worthy student to compensate for the financial loss. The egregore shifts. Her remaining students are no longer just students; they're also customers with expectations. This is usually quite subtle, but every now and then it flares up and disrupts the group dynamic. In time, the quality of Glinda's initiates changes, as their ability to pay becomes a consideration. As those initiates go on to start their own covens, adopting Glinda's business model, Flying Cat Wicca as a whole feels the impact.

What would Wicca look like if coven leaders only accepted students with the ability to pay for it? If initiation could ultimately be purchased? It is absolutely reasonable for skilled laborers to demand payment, but Wicca is a priesthood, not a commodity. The gods do not only call those with expendable income. A traditional Wiccan may charge for her services as a Witch (though many refuse this, also)—for readings, for spellwork, for public lectures or workshops—but not for her power to pass her lineage and bring others before the gods of her tradition. This cannot be bought and sold. Period. Over the years, especially as other types of Witchcraft have come to include training fees, this has become increasingly taboo in traditional Wicca. Within wider Witchcraft communities, charging students may be more commonplace and accepted, but traditional Wiccan priests and priestesses will never require monetary compensation. It's true, however, that coven leaders often incur a cost, and this can be difficult to manage without help. There are many ways to lighten the load that don't involve a payment contract. Initiates may (and often do) help with the financial burden of running a group by bringing ritual supplies, food to share, or other incidentals. But if a potential coven leader opens by explaining their payment options, politely excuse yourself and continue seeking.

They spend a lot of time trashing other covens or individuals in the community.

The truth is, Witches and Pagans don't always get along with everyone. Over time, we all meet practitioners that we don't like. Other groups in the area may do things we don't agree with. We may run into individual practitioners who just aren't very nice or who we don't respect for whatever reason. That's pretty natural, and it's okay to not get along with every person you meet. What's *not* okay is making that discontent the focus of your *own* Witchcraft. When a coven leader (or a whole coven) seems to constantly be embroiled in some kind of community melodrama, proceed with caution. The more time someone spends tangled up in a Witch war, the less time they have to actually practice Witchcraft. This works both ways: if the people you're considering constantly trash talk others, that's often indicative of some shortcoming of their own. At the same time, if you hear *other* Witches consistently badmouthing the group you're considering, pay attention. Sometimes rumors are just rumors, but a bad reputation doesn't usually just spring from nothing. Be fair and form your own opinions, but go in with your eyes open.

They immediately try to wow you with talk of their hard-to-believe magical exploits.

Far be it from me to declare where the boundaries of magic fall. I've seen some pretty incredible things in my twenty years of Craft practice, and my policy is generally to give other people the benefit of the doubt. If someone tells me that their magic has cured terminal illness and that they regularly descend to the underworld to confront death directly, I'm going to smile politely, nod, and trust that whatever they think they're experiencing is meaningful for them, regardless of my own opinion. Hey, some of the stuff I believe sounds ridiculous to plenty of other people. Join the club. But if you're getting the impression that the people you're talking to are telling you things specifically to impress you, beware. There are a lot of insecure folks in the world, and there are plenty of Witches of all stripes who spend most of their energy just trying to convince others that they're stronger, more serious, more innately powerful, or otherwise "realer" than anyone else. But magic is as personal as it is inexplicable. It's a great act of trust to share it with outsiders. When strangers immediately divulge seemingly impossible (or, hey, *actually* impossible) accomplishments, you're likely just listening to a lot of hot air.

They proposition you.

Witches don't generally shy away from talk of sex, but there are still boundaries. The relationship between seeker and coven leader represents a significant power differential, and this raises questions surrounding consent. It's one thing for a mutual attraction to develop between equals, but it's quite another to rely on one's authority as a group leader to pressure someone else into sex. There are people in the world who use the Craft—and their position in the Craft—to take advantage of others (and, let's just be direct, especially young women). Listen to your instincts here. It's true that Wicca may emphasize sexual themes and that individual Witches may engage in sexual rites as part of their personal practices. It's also true that Wicca tends to attract people who may be more sexually open. There's nothing wrong with this. However, at no point do you sacrifice your right to your own body. Very few of us ever find ourselves in these positions (and most would be horrified), but predators exist in every community. If you feel threatened or pressured, leave. You always have that right.

 FROM THE CIRCLE

Sex is personal. Don't confuse it with spirituality. No-fraternization rules (for example, between officers and enlisted, between coworkers in the same department, or between professors and college students) exist for good reason. There's an imbalance of perceived power, authority, or knowledge. In one instance I experienced, a student waited until a year's classes were complete before broaching a teacher with a personal attraction. That's a responsible student.

—*Deb Snavely, New Wiccan Church, International*

The lives of coven leaders or students seem to just generally be out of order.

Figuring this one out can take some time. There's no perfect standard that everyone in a coven has to meet. No one's life is perfect. Everyone falls short sometimes. People struggle financially. People get sick. People have relationship problems. We lose our jobs, we deal with death, we make poor choices, and we all do things that we regret. Everyone's life goes to shit sometimes, and this includes Witches. But if the coven seems to be in a constant state of turmoil—especially to the point where the emotional or financial health of students is affected—continue cautiously. It's true that everyone deals with hardship, but it's also true that misery loves company. I've seen situations where covens have collapsed thanks to eviction, divorce, drug abuse, and a number of other ills. Sometimes it's not possible to set aside personal troubles for the sake of students. Sometimes the most responsible thing for a leader to do is put the coven on hiatus. Whatever the case, your focus should be on your own spiritual pursuits, not on the personal problems of your would-be high priestess or high priest. Do not commit to the care of others beyond your capacity to do so and at the expense of your own training.

In finding the perfect coven, there are few hard-and-fast rules. Many will take exception to some of the things I'm calling red flags. Whatever you decide for yourself, remember: you are a seeker, not a child. Do not surrender your personal authority and do not ignore your own good judgment. You can walk away from a situation at any time, for any reason, and owe no one an explanation. Very few of the people you meet will want anything but the best for you. Mostly, you will encounter good, sincere, trustworthy people. But it is naïve to assume that everyone in any community deserves your trust. There are many kinds of predators in the world, and traditional Wicca is not immune to their presence. There's no need to be paranoid, but there is always cause to be cautious and smart.

When You're Told No

Sometimes, things just won't work out the way you think they should. Maybe you'll hear nothing, despite a well-crafted seeker letter and all the sincerest intentions. Maybe you received a reply … just not the one you wanted. Sometimes, the answer is no, despite our worthiness and despite our good efforts. This can be a very discouraging experience, if not a genuinely heartbreaking one.

I have turned away more than one worthy seeker with deep-felt regret. In almost every case, my reasoning had nothing to do with them. I was simply overwhelmed with the initiates and students that I already had, and I couldn't commit to taking anyone else on. Foxfire has always been a small group—most covens are—and we just don't have the manpower (Witchpower?) to open our circle to every qualified person who finds us. When I commit to something, I do so wholeheartedly. If I know that I don't have the energy or time to do right by the person or the project, I won't accept that responsibility. I believe it's better to wait and produce quality rather than settle and hope for the best. In such cases, I encourage seekers to stay in touch, get involved in the local community, and, if I can, I will point them to other covens that may be able to help them along their paths.

There are many reasons why a coven may tell you to look elsewhere. While I will turn away seekers when I feel that my coven may become larger than we can handle, others may only bring newcomers in during particular seasons. The period between Halloween and the winter solstice is often regarded as a "dark period"—the time between the end of the old year and the beginning of the new, when the world lies fallow—and some coven leaders will abstain from beginning new projects. This includes taking on new students or performing initiations. The timing may simply not be right. Individual covens may have their own seasonal cycles dictating when they are open to new members, and you may simply not be privy to this detail. Try again in a few months! You may receive a very different answer.

It's also common that a coven leader decides that a seeker's personality, inclinations, or lifestyle simply doesn't fit in with the group as a whole. There is a balance to be struck here, of course. Differences can make a coven stronger, but they can also cause unnecessary discomfort or strife if they are in overt conflict with the existing egregore or even the tradition itself. To give you an example, I once referred a seeker elsewhere because he was a vegan who also abstained from alcohol. Don't get me wrong—there's nothing to say you can't be a vegan and practice Wicca or that you must consume alcohol. Many traditional Wiccans share in one or both of these choices. My decision was based purely on practicality and the individual character of my specific coven. Alcohol is an ever-present feature of our rituals, and certain beverages are routinely employed in sacred devotional offering to our gods. We were not willing to eliminate this practice to accommodate a newcomer—our gods and our personal traditions took precedence. As for his veganism, again, that might be very appropriate in another coven setting, but not in Foxfire. I am a licensed hunter, and the use of certain animal parts is a central component of Foxfire's magical praxis. While I take no issue with the beliefs of others, I understand that my own are reprehensible to some, and this seeker was clearly one such person. He could not reasonably have been expected to be content circling with us. This was not a reflection on his fit for Wicca—only for a single coven. He was not a good match for Foxfire, and we were an equally poor fit for him. No hard feelings! There are many other traditional covens out there, and I knew that he would find another that would serve him better than we could. When I told him so, it was not my intention to disparage his character or his personal choices. Whether or not he agreed with me in the moment, I knew he would be unhappy with us, and we would struggle with him.

This is just one such story I could tell. You may be excluded because of your age (most covens will require you to have at least reached the age of legal adulthood, but many have restrictions beyond even that), your particular proclivities (maybe you're really interested in New Age spiritual practices and the coven in question is strictly rooted in European Paganisms), your past experiences, your educational background, your profession, whether or not you have children or are married, or one of many other possibilities. Some of these are more reasonable than others, of course. Like it or not, a coven may base their decision on any criteria they choose, and you as the seeker will probably never know. Individual covens, as always, will draw their own lines.

It's a sad truth that there are groups that will exclude based on race, gender identity, sexuality, socioeconomic class, and other such factors. Some groups will exclude seekers based on misunderstandings about disabilities, mental illness, and similar considerations. As someone who has struggled with mental illness, I have experienced such things firsthand. When I was a seeker, I always tried to be upfront about my past difficulties with depression, anxiety, and self-injury. I knew there would be no hiding it, and, further, I didn't think I should have to keep it secret (some of my scars are quite significant, so there was no hope of hiding in a skyclad circle, anyway). I met coven leaders who believed that I was inherently unsuited to be a priestess. In subsequent years, I've met a handful of others who will say disparaging things about the suitability of people who take antidepressants, completely unaware that they're speaking to someone who relies on medication herself (people and their assumptions, I tell you what). And this kind of prejudice often pales in comparison to that faced by people of color, the genderqueer, the physically disabled, and others who defy long-standing expectations and assumptions. While, thankfully, prejudice is increasingly uncommon and new generations of Witches are working hard to combat it, it's not impossible that you will encounter it. If you do, remind yourself that you're valuable, you deserve the same consideration as everyone else, and you are not responsible for the ignorance of others. Keep seeking. There is a coven out there that will value the person that you are.

When you are not invited to circle with a particular coven, it's also possible that the leaders you spoke with decided that you simply weren't ready. Training in a traditional coven is a heavy commitment that alters the daily course of your life. Remember, this is a priesthood. You are not simply joining a congregation or a casual study group. Beyond simply having to rearrange your calendar, belonging to a coven will impact your relationships with your current friends and family, and it will change the way you move about in the world. When practitioners say that Witchcraft is dangerous, this is part of what they mean. Practicing the Craft changes you. You will view the world differently. You will interact with outsiders differently. The things you value may change. The way you think may change. It's one thing to be curious about magic and to want to learn about Wicca. It's quite another to be called to enter the priesthood *of* the Wica.

Even when you understand that, it may still be difficult to realize that you aren't quite where you need to be in life to undertake that step. Often, coven leaders will look for indicators of a high level of stability: a steady job or school routine, a stable marriage or contented singlehood, a secure home life, a good sense of who you are in the world, and many other factors that we would associate with a certain level of maturity. These are the most obvious. It is difficult to be successful beginning in a traditional coven when you're in the middle of a divorce, when you're newly pregnant with your first child, when you're struggling with medical school applications, when you're considering moving cross-country, or when you've just lost your job and are terrified of what to do next. These are usually bad times to take on *any* major commitment beyond what is already at hand. On the other hand, sometimes periods of transition are *perfect* for undergoing dramatic life change. Sometimes upheaval can work in your favor and create the space necessary to start anew. Everyone is different. You must know yourself. The high priestess or high priest considering you must base their decision on initial impressions of you, as well as their own past experiences with others in positions similar to yours. Only half of that is in your control.

Regardless of why you are told no, the correct response is twofold. First, do a self-check. Be honest with yourself. Was this really the right time? Was this the right coven? The right tradition? Is this something you can actually help by doing something different next time? Or is there something else at work that is beyond you? Second—if you can still feel that calling inside of yourself—keep practicing Witchcraft. Keep learning. Keep trying things. Keep growing. Listen to yourself and talk to the gods and spirits. Now may be the right time, for whatever reason, but that time will come. Be ready. Remember, too, that you are only one half of this equation. You must also decide when a coven is or is not right for you. Evaluate potential leaders sternly and be discerning. Accept an invitation to join because you believe it may be the right place for you, not because it is the only offer on the table. This is about *you*, not just the needs of any one coven. Everyone takes their own time and walks their own path, even when they're part of a tradition or a coven. You can't rush things, even when you try.

CHAPTER 9

SUCCEEDING IN AN OUTER COURT

Even after several lengthy email exchanges, phone calls, and numerous cups of coffee, it's very unlikely that you'll receive a direct offer of initiation. Too much is at stake to bring someone in so casually, as you've seen. With so many new people exploring Witchcraft every year and an always-growing variety of traditions and types emerging, it's increasingly important for coven leaders to ensure that potential members are a good fit for the group. Individual covens may employ very different strategies for doing this, but most traditional groups rely on an outer court, sometimes called a training circle, a grove, or a Pagan group.

Outer court performs several key functions. At the most basic level, it creates an environment where coven members and seekers can build relationships, getting to know each other and building trust. It also provides a space for newcomers to the Craft (or, at least, to the Craft as it's practiced by that coven) to begin to learn the ropes. Outer court is a proving ground where everyone has the opportunity to determine fit, both between the coven and the seeker and between the coven and the tradition itself. A newcomer may be a good match for one and a poor match for the other. Outer court also allows newcomers to learn the necessary skills of Witchcraft in an environment that entails less commitment and less magical intensity than a circle of initiates.

Outer court may take several forms. Usually, it is a ritual group all its own, with a liturgy that doesn't require the swearing of oaths or the revealing of secret texts. Seekers may experience the bones of Wiccan practice without being prematurely exposed to its inner Mysteries. They may also learn magical techniques that will build a foundation for fluency in inner court. Some outer courts emphasize discussion and reading over formal ritual. Seekers may complete a more literary curriculum, reading assigned books, writing essays, and participating in academic conversations about topics related to Witchcraft and other occult traditions. You may encounter a combination of these things as well. Both models (and potentially others) allow coven leaders to measure the appropriateness of individual seekers and provide opportunities for growth.

Outer court represents a critical period in the Craft lives of most seekers. These are some of your most important years as a Witch (yes, *years*—more on that in a minute). As with all things in the Craft, your path is your own and your experiences will be unique, but there are absolutely steps that you can take to ensure that you succeed in outer court. The truth is that many seekers never make it beyond this phase, for a variety of reasons. Getting that first invitation is a momentous event worth celebrating, but the work is really only just beginning.

A Year and a Day ... At Least

In eclectic Wiccan communities, there is a custom of studying the Craft for a year and a day before choosing to commit to a life of practice. Many beginner's books are actually structured with this in mind, organizing lessons designed to walk students through a complete turn of the Wheel of the Year, at the end of which they may perform a personal dedication ritual. If you've spent much time in online Pagan communities, you may have heard people say things like, "I'm in the middle of my year and a day," or "I'm going to start my year and a day next month," or some such, as though this was some kind of perfunctory step that was just an inherent part of becoming a Witch. While this practice may be common, the custom of waiting a year and a day for initiation is not a universal Wiccan imperative. Many traditional groups have no such requirement (and you might even get a chuckle or two if you ask).

The timeframe of a year and a day has European cultural significance stemming from multiple sources. In certain occult fraternities—for example, Freemasonry—this really is a set length of time where an apprentice must wait for initiation. Dating from at least the mid-sixteenth century, English common law has maintained the "year and a day rule" in homicide cases, which states that death as the result of a wrongful act (for example, abuse or neglect) must occur within the period of a year and a day in order to be considered murder. Finally, there is religious weight to this timeframe thanks to its use in the retelling of certain European myths—for example, the story of the Witch Cerridwen, who must brew her famous wisdom-granting potion for a year and a day. Over time, in popular usage, this expression has also come to mean "forever," or perhaps "as long as it takes," in the same way that the number ten thousand is often used to mean "countless" or "infinity" in Chinese cultures. Regardless of where it comes from, with the circulation of popular books and the growth of the internet, the idea that neophyte Wiccans must spend a year and a day studying prior to initiation has become standardized.

As a new outer court student, however, this is the first bit of misinformation you'll need to abandon. Because building trust is one of the central tasks of an outer court and because individual seekers come to the Craft with greater and lesser degrees of preparedness, the length of time prior to initiation often varies significantly from seeker to seeker. You may very well encounter a group that adheres to a year-and-a-day policy for potential members, but even in these cases this is usually understood to be a *minimum*, not a literal three hundred and sixty-six days. According to whatever criteria the coven sets, leaders may be able to make a decision about your fit in only a few weeks. If they are interested in your familiarity with certain esoteric subjects or your

149

ability to work certain kinds of ritual effectively, then a particularly experienced seeker may only require a short experience in outer court. A total newbie may take several years.

Belonging to a coven is a major commitment, and it sometimes takes significant amounts of time to adjust. Some covens may send you away and tell you to come back when your life is more conducive to that commitment. Others may be very flexible and patient, allowing for a more gradual transition. I have personally met seekers whom I knew almost immediately belonged in our tradition and deserved a prompt initiation. I've met others who clearly weren't ready but had so much potential that it was worth accommodating them and taking things slowly. My very first initiates spent almost two years in outer court simply because *I* was the one who needed to figure out if I was ready to be a high priestess. A number of considerations may be at work here.

Whatever the case, take this to heart: outer court takes as long as it takes. Lasting beyond a year doesn't entitle you to initiation. You will not automatically be initiated simply for showing up over the course of a designated timeframe. It's not time by itself that's important, but the effort you put into that time and the growth that results. Some seekers come to outer court already primed for initiatory work. Others need the experience of celebrating a full turn of the Wheel of the Year. Still others must significantly restructure their lives, addressing long-term personal issues that affect Craft work. These seekers may stay in outer court for two or three years. It is very likely that you will experience impatience. It is very likely that a time will come when you won't understand what's taking so long. You may even watch as other students with less time under their belts move ahead of you. Many people have this experience, and it can be painful (it happens in inner court, too, so think of this as practice). Remind yourself: this takes as long as it takes. You're not in competition with anyone (including yourself). At best, a year and a day is a guideline or perhaps even a minimum. Do not make the mistake of getting overly hung up on how long things take. You can't rush, and there isn't a cosmic time limit.

 FROM THE CIRCLE

In my tradition, initiation is never offered. You must ask for it. That sometimes includes even asking to be initiated multiple times in order to test your fortitude. So after a number of years, I decided to request initiation. I was initiated into the Wicca very quickly after that since I had already been through what may be described as the "probationary period." The coven was actually relived that I finally decided to ask for initiation, because they said they had been sitting on their hands just waiting for me to ask them the whole time! I haven't looked back since!

—*Thorn Nightwind, priest of the Horsa and Sacred Pentagraph traditions*

Becoming Clergy

Beyond hierarchy, beyond the coven structure, and beyond initiation rituals, the fundamental difference between traditional Wicca and many other kinds of Paganism and Witchcraft is that this is a priesthood. When you commit to an outer court, what you're really doing is exploring the calling to be a priest or priestess of the gods of the Wica. If you are only interested in learning to practice magic or just think it would be cool to call yourself a Witch, this is not the place for you. It's okay to be curious. It's okay to want to explore magic for magic's sake. It's okay to be concerned about self-improvement. It's okay to want to learn coveted secrets and histories. Sometimes that's how a calling begins—with something simpler. But the seekers who earn initiation—and who ultimately go on to serve their communities as coven leaders in their own right—come to understand that Wicca is more than a skill set. It's not a bandage for a crumbling personal life or a distraction for when you're bored. You're not joining a sports team or signing up for a class at the local community center. This is not the place for the merely curious. If you're asking to be part of a coven, those leaders are assuming that you're knowingly preparing for a significant life change. That's what a traditional Wiccan initiation is: a significant life change. Joining an outer court—no matter the tradition or personal style of the leaders—will require some life rearrangement of one kind or another. Your priorities will likely shift. Beginning a formal study of Wicca is thrilling. You start to see things differently and experience the world differently. It can also be somewhat traumatic, though, in that it represents a major change that will impact practically every arena of your life. That's why the vetting process often begins with questions about your personal life; your personal life impacts your outer court training just as much if not more than your spiritual life.

My personal experience has been that when seekers don't make it through outer court training, it's usually because they are unable to commit to the time requirements and to the rebalancing that traditional Wicca demands. What happens when your spouse doesn't understand the amount of time you're suddenly spending with your new coven (who may be total strangers, as far as your spouse is concerned)? Can you train in a coven without compromising your responsibilities as a parent? Will your job schedule be steady enough that you can attend regular coven events? What about your school schedule? How will you handle friends who don't understand why you suddenly can't share this part of your life with them as openly as you might like? These are very challenging concerns! Some will impact you more than others (and there are plenty more that I haven't even included). It's impossible to anticipate everything you'll have to face, and every seeker's experience is different. As you begin to move forward, one of the best things you can do for yourself is to strive to achieve some kind of balance between your mundane and magical lives.

It's hard to say where the boundary between the ordinary and the magical lies. On the one hand, beginning a new life in the Craft is exciting and can feel delightfully overwhelming. It's understandable to want to escape into more enchanted realms. It's very easy to become consumed by your occult explorations. There's so much to learn and so much to try! And when you're surrounded by more experienced covenmates—Witches who may have decades, if not lifetimes, more practice than you—it's easy to feel like you've got to catch up. *You don't.* Because the other hand is this: your life has always been magical. That divide between magic and mundanity is constructed. Many of the skills and experiences that will best serve you as a new Witch are things that you've already acquired just by surviving in the world: creativity, patience, resourcefulness, perseverance, and balance. That last one is especially important. Your Craft life and your personal life are not distinct things. You can't neglect one for the other. Likewise, when you nurture one, you feed the other.

As a new student in an outer court, part of what you're responsible for is learning the histories and mechanics of a new tradition. There will be plenty to read and discuss and memorize and understand. But just as important—and potentially quite a bit more challenging—is figuring out where and how the Craft intermingles with and fuels the rest of your life. You can't practice Witchcraft in a vacuum! If you're like most people, you don't have the luxury of infinite free time to devote however you choose. You go to work, go to school, run a household, are responsible for other family members, and have all kinds of social and professional obligations on top of all that. If you're not careful, it's easy for your spirituality to start feeling like a luxury item that sometimes you just can't afford. Beyond learning the basics and getting to know your new group, finding this balance is one of the biggest hurdles faced by new outer court students.

One strategy is to take those things in your life—especially those things that you love, those things that make you who you are—and turn them into devotional acts. If you're an athlete, a craftsperson, an artist, a soldier, a writer, a teacher, an organizer, a parent (and the list goes on), see if there's a way you can bring elements of your new Craft into those realms. My own writing is very much an act of worship, connecting me to the gods I serve. The act of putting pen to paper, whether in a private journal or for the sake of a piece I intend to share with a large audience, is as magical as casting a circle or performing a spell. It *is* a spell. I may not be burning candles or wafting incense, but my writing is an act of Witchcraft. This very book is the result of intense magical work. I've always been a writer, but becoming a Witch taught me to make writing an act of both Will and devotion to the gods. That's just me. For you, it might be your athletic training or the time you spend in your garden. Maybe it's something simpler, like how you organize your planner at the beginning of each week or the conscious effort you put into cleaning your home.

Beyond enchanting the things I already did, my developing relationships with the gods led me to explore completely new activities. An increasingly intense series of encounters with the Horned God drew me to archery and, eventually, to traditional bowhunting. It occurred to me that, if I wanted to build a deeper connection with him, it made sense to try exploring his realm, meeting him on his own terms. For me, that meant learning to hunt and experiencing the relationship between life and death in a way that most urban Pagans do not. My physical abilities and local resources (I live in a place where deer hunting is both a rich cultural practice and critical to the local ecology) allowed me to pursue this calling to unusual ends—most devotees to gods of the hunt do not feel compelled to literally begin hunting, nor should we expect this. You will have your own encounters, in your own time. Begin listening. You may find yourself in some very surprising places.

Of course, it's easier to find enchantment in those activities that already bring us pleasure and make us feel centered. Finding it in hard work, monotony, loneliness, and pain is significantly harder (and perhaps this isn't something we should even aspire to do at all times). Honestly, this is something that never stops being a struggle. Being a Witch doesn't mean your whole life becomes easy. You'll still have to pay taxes, deal with coworkers you don't like, manage illness and injury, wrangle an overloaded schedule, and figure out how you're going to pay your car repair bill. That's always going to be true. Life will continue to be hard, and frequently unfair.

But Wicca gives you one more tool in your toolbox. When you struggle, you may find comfort and reassurance in your connection to the gods and to your covenmates. To address practical matters you may employ magic. To address those things that seem too heavy to carry on your own, you may turn to a whole network of fellow practitioners to ask for support. Sometimes that's all we need. Witches experience the ups and downs of life just the same as everyone else does, but our traditions provide us with emotional and spiritual resources that can smooth them. Wicca won't automatically fix everything that's gone wrong in your life—nothing can do that—but it can help to give some of those things further context and meaning and provide structure to process, heal, and grow.

 FROM THE CIRCLE

My eight-year-old doesn't know, but he periodically says he thinks I'm a Witch (which is adorable and disconcerting). I'm happy with him figuring things out on his own, and he knows he's always welcome to my library. He knows he can ask me anything and I'll give him an honest answer. I want him to find his own path in life, however, whatever that looks like. With my husband, it was trickier in the beginning. My husband was raised Catholic and became atheist/agnostic-ish in high school. When I first got consumed with learning about Wicca, he was understandably worried that I was going to be "some kind of born-again religious nut." This wasn't too far off in some ways ... I really *did* feel born again, and a little nutty. It took a lot of frank conversations with him for me to balance things.

—*Wren, first degree priestess*

Meeting Your Shadow

All of this brings us to another important point. Traditional Wiccan training can bring out the best in you, but it will also reveal you at your worst. Craft practice requires an intense, ongoing examination of the self, and that means addressing those things that may be hurting us or preventing us from growing into the people we wish to become. Effective Witchcraft requires a deep understanding of your own character. Who are you? What experiences have made you who you are? What do you want out of your life? How do you relate to others? What are you afraid of? What truly makes you happy? Are you doing what you can to take responsibility for your own life?

Some of these questions sound simple but in reality are quite profound. Most of us would like to think that we're reflective, self-aware people, but the truth is that real self-examination is frequently a very painful process. In many New Age and Pagan communities, this kind of psychological, emotional exploration is called "shadow work," in reference to the work of psychiatrist Carl Jung (1875–1961), who saw the "shadow" as those parts of the personality that are unconscious or hidden. Shadow work pushes us to confront those parts of ourselves that exist in darkness. These are things that we aren't conscious of at all, things that we may be ashamed of, things that we keep secret, or things that we wish not to acknowledge.

Self-knowledge is one of the cornerstones of the Western Magical Tradition (really a group of traditions), which birthed Wicca. Preparation for initiation into the Mysteries demands that we confront our shadows. Whether you like it or not and whether or not it's what you intend, beginning in outer court and preparing for initiation will dredge up those parts of your psyche that usually go unexamined. It may be sooner or it may be later, but eventually you will have to deal with your personal issues. Whatever those issues are—whether it's your childhood trauma, your string of bad relationships, your unaddressed depression, or your tendency to gossip—they're going to get in the way if they go ignored. Your covenmates aren't licensed counselors (well, probably) and circle isn't therapy, but just the process of engaging in the rites and working Wiccan magic in the presence of our gods has a way of bringing out all the components of who we are and making us look at them. This is one of the Mysteries, and it often begins in outer court. The experience is hard, but it's also liberating. When you master the shadow (insofar as we ever can), it stops being terrifying, shameful, or confusing.

Traditional Wicca has many varieties and individual covens may be very different, but you know it's real and right when it transforms you for the better. Really, it never stops transforming you. Each stage poses its own challenges. Many of the things I had to learn and deal with in outer court I still struggle with as a high priestess. You won't necessarily slay your dragons, but you're guaranteed at least to meet them.

An Outer Court Checklist

Beyond the intensity of spiritual development and your encounters with the inexplicable Mysteries, thriving in an outer court and ultimately earning a permanent place in a coven is a very practical matter. You have little to no control over whether or not you fit in with the group's egregore—and that you'll discover in time—but you have complete control over your personal comportment and the effort you put into the work before you. There are very tangible things that you can do or not do that will impact the likelihood of your being ultimately offered initiation and, more importantly, getting the most out of your time in outer court. Here are some general rules of thumb that will apply within most traditional covens:

1. Do what you say you'll do.
It sounds clear enough, but this makes a huge statement about your character, and many fall short here. If you tell your high priestess, high priest, or covenmates that you'll do something, do it. That means

arriving to meetings on time, completing the tasks that you commit to, bringing what you say you'll bring, and generally displaying your integrity. Part of the Witch's power lies in her words. If yours are meaningless, then your Craft will be, too. If your potential coven's leaders have cause to think you unreliable, your days in outer court are numbered. But beyond just that, you'll be halting your own personal growth. Wicca's emphasis on doing and experiencing, rather than belief, in and of itself means that you get out of it what you put in. You can't develop as a Witch if you don't practice and you don't do your homework. This means exploring on your own as well as doing whatever tasks your Craft teachers ask of you. You may be required to read particular books, write a short paper on some magical topic, perform particular rituals or meditations, or potentially any number of other worthwhile activities. Do the work in order to reap the rewards.

 FROM THE CIRCLE

I expect my outer court students to attend all agreed-upon classes and circles. I expect then to communicate if questions or concerns come up. I expect them to be independent enough to look for answers other than mine. I require a willingness to work at Craft. That may mean reading, writing, doing personal ritual, or meditation. I'm not usually looking for "freshmen." I want "seniors" or "graduate students."
—*Deb Snavely, New Wiccan Church, International*

2. Contribute to the group.

You're not solitary anymore. As a member of an outer court, you've got a responsibility to other people, as well as additional responsibility to yourself. Pitch in to cover meals, perishable ritual supplies, and other material necessaries. There's a very serious taboo in traditional Wicca against accepting money for training, but a cost is still incurred by coven leaders. Bottles of wine, extra toilet paper, pre- and postritual meals, candles, and incense are not free. It's extremely unlikely that you'll be asked for cash at any point in your training, but you'll probably be expected to contribute to the stock of items required to run the group. Even if you're never asked, it's polite to always show up to circle with something in hand. There's no need to put yourself out; small things are always welcome. Consider bringing a plate of cookies or cakes for ritual, a bottle of wine to share, a side dish for dinner, or an extra roll of paper towels. If you're really short on cash one month, do something to help around the house. Take out the trash generated by the coven that evening, or wash the dishes after dinner. There are lots of ways to be helpful, and your efforts will be both noticed and appreciated.

Beyond those tangible things, it's just as important that you contribute your voice! Share your thoughts and experiences. When the time comes to discuss a ritual, a book, or an idea, don't sit there like a lump. Even if you're not sure what you think, you're still processing, or you want to wait until a more private moment away from the whole group, make sure you find a way to express yourself. You're not an observer, just there to sit silently and absorb the efforts of other people. Be active. Bring your brain along with that pack of toilet paper.

3. Talk to your leaders.

Your new high priestess or high priest is not a mind reader. However magical they may be, they can't simply look into your eyes once a month at circle and instantly know your deepest hopes and thoughts. They also can't know your work schedule. You need to actually communicate with them. That's your responsibility, not theirs. Very few high priestesses or high priests will go out of their way to track you down like a schoolteacher collecting homework. If you show up to circle but then vanish in between, your coven leaders will assume that you either lack serious interest or the time to commit to a working coven. Be sure you're reaching out and keeping the people in charge informed when they need to be. This is practical—they need to know if you're not going to be in attendance or if your job is suddenly eating your life—but also spiritual.

Much of the learning you'll do takes place outside of formal ritual, in one-on-one conversations with your high priest or priestess and other elders. So call them. Hang out with them. Be available. Share your life and build strong relationships.

4. Don't compete.

There's something about people that seems to just make us naturally competitive. We compete at work, at school, and in practically every other aspect of our lives. We strive to be wealthier, to be more attractive, to have more followers on social media, better sexual partners, better clothes, and more rigorous workout routines. We even compete in suffering (have you ever told someone about an illness or injury and then listened while they immediately responded with something even worse that happened to them?). Whether it's something deep in our monkey brains, powered by evolution, or the result of the aggressive market environment that we live in, we often feel like we need to out-do the people around us. That extends to even our practice of the Craft. We show off on social media and at open rituals and festivals, competing to be the most authentic, the most established, the most knowledgeable, to have the most students, the most books, and whatever else. In some ways, being in a tradition with a degree system can make that competitive tendency particularly likely to show. It's really, really easy to feel like you have to keep up with your coven siblings, or even to beat them, as though you were racing. And even if you're genuinely only focusing on yourself, it's easy to hold yourself to some impossible standard of where you should be and what you should know. This is still competitive thinking. This kind of attitude is great if you're striving for valedictorian or to make partner at your firm, but it's terrible for a coven student (and worse for an initiated priest or priestess).

You are not in competition with *anyone.*

You will learn at your own pace. You will process your experiences at your own pace. You will not become an effective Witch because you can out-read, out-speak, or out-buy another student. Though I admire diligence and academic rigor (I'm very bookish myself, so I can appreciate these qualities in others), as a coven leader, I'm not going to hold one student above another because they can read faster or write a better essay. I also don't care if your athame cost more, if you can meditate twice as long, or you've been practicing since you were a kid while someone else didn't start until they were in their fifties. I don't have an initiation quota I have to meet, and neither do your own coven leaders. Take your time. Be yourself. Do what's best for you. Your own progress is not a statement about anyone else, nor is their progress a statement about you.

5. Shut up.

There's a time and a place for talking about your Craft and your work in your new outer court. It's exciting, and it's natural to want to share your excitement with others, but now is the time to begin practicing discernment and restraint. Every coven makes its own decision about how public they wish to make their Craft. Some groups maintain social media profiles and are very active in public Pagan communities. Others are extremely private, following the older tradition of not even revealing their legal names to covenmates and actively denying Craft involvement outside of ritual space. But on whichever end of the spectrum you may find yourself, it's best to begin with discretion. The ability to remain silent is important in traditional Wiccan spaces, and your coven leaders need to be able to trust that you can keep sensitive experiences and information to yourself. If everything you learn in private ends up online or in the mouths of outsiders, your high priestess and high priest are going to decide that you aren't fit for inner court. Always err on the side of silence. That doesn't necessarily mean lying to your friends or denying your Craft. In time, you'll learn to avoid compromising situations, to redirect nosey questions, and to answer outside curiosities in ways that are polite and satisfying without being overly revealing. This is a skill acquired in time and with practice, and initially the boundaries can be quite fuzzy. Talk to your teachers about what is and isn't appropriate. When you're unsure, shut your mouth.

Keep these relatively simple things in mind and always be honest with yourself and with your new group, and you will avoid most of the major pitfalls that get many seekers and first-time group members into trouble. Instead, you can focus on learning and answering those more fundamental questions: Is this the group for me? Is this the tradition where I belong? Am I getting something valuable out of this?

Remember, if you're not enjoying yourself this early in the game, it's okay to look for alternatives. Many seekers end up in very different places from where they started. As serious as this endeavor is, it should also be fun. A strong outer court will prepare you for the work of inner court. You'll learn to work in a group (which can be quite challenging if you've always been solitary) and begin to build relationships with people who will come to feel like family. You'll develop the magical and ritual skills that will create the foundation for initiatory work. You'll come to know yourself more honestly and intimately. You'll begin to have inklings of what it means to know the gods. You'll probably struggle at some point. You'll get frustrated. There will be tears. But outer court done well will make you a more capable, more self-aware (and therefore more powerful) Witch. Enjoy the work. Do it well.

FROM THE CIRCLE

Outer court is like one of those survival shows in which contestants start out with a fire, but then they have to move. So they create a smolder bundle to carry an ember to start a second fire at their next camp. In circle, you get that ember, and you have to take it home. You have to nurture it and build your own fire away from the covenstead. If you do nothing with it, it will die.

—*Rayn, Gardnerian high priestess*

CHAPTER 10
SOME GUIDANCE FOR THE NEW INITIATE

Seeking is hard. Finding the right coven can take years—there's no two ways about it. You'll have false starts. You'll hit walls. You'll write beautiful introductory emails and hear crickets. You'll have awkward coffee dates with strangers. You'll go to terrible open rituals and public meetups that leave you feeling isolated and out of place. Believe me, those of us who've been at this for decades know how frustrating things can be. But diligence pays off. If you truly look, if you take risks, stay honest with yourself and with others, and if you're patient, you will find your way to the edge of the circle. Maybe you picked up this book because you're already in a traditional coven or a traditional outer court and you just wanted another perspective, or some additional insight into some aspect of your tradition. Perhaps you've been working through this guide all the way from square one, and you find yourself finally on the other side—a new initiate! In that case, congratulations! Initiation marks the culmination of a lot of hard work (and the beginning of much more) and is a truly remarkable achievement. This chapter is for you, though it will also apply to both outer court students and longtime initiates who may just need the reminder.

In magical communities, we speak often of the Four Powers of the Magus. If you've been hanging out in Wiccan spaces for long, you probably know them as the corners of the Witch's Pyramid: to know, to dare, to will, and to be silent. These are the pillars of many Western magical systems, corresponding to the four elements and the four cardinal directions. When we lack one, our Work becomes weak. When in doubt or in need of direction, it's useful to return to these basic tenets.

To Know

Acacia kneeled before the altar, holding her athame's hilt against her chest. It was a big night for her. She was acting as high priestess for the evening and was responsible for her very first group ritual. All eyes were on her, and the time had come to consecrate the salt. Up until that point she'd done quite well. Lukaos and I stood with the other students, relinquishing our usual leadership roles to give Acacia the opportunity to practice her freshly acquired skills. She commanded the space well and had clearly worked hard to memorize the ritual. She was confident, handling the sword like she was born to it (because she was). But all of a sudden, the candlelight flickering across her face, she hesitated. A moment too many passed and her eyes snapped to mine, panicked, silently screaming. I could read her face instantly because I'd been exactly there a hundred times: *Oh shit. What comes next?*

"Take a breath. The words are in there," I said in a low tone across the altar.

Another moment passed. She took a deep breath, but still nothing came. She looked at me again.

"You're a Witch. Forget about the script. Consecrate the salt."

Acacia took another breath—this one stern—and her face shifted. She relaxed visibly. The words that came next weren't the ones on the page she'd spent so long trying to recall, but they were magical and right nonetheless. She forgot, yes, but she knew the essence of what she was doing, so the power wasn't lost.

There are multiple ways to know things. In the heat of the moment, it's easy to forget a memorized passage, and some people struggle more than others with this kind of rote learning. On the one hand, a rustling paper can be a distraction, taking away from the beauty and drama of ritual. On the other hand, the real power lies in the intention behind the words. If a Witch can generate that power while reading, then why shouldn't she? Power exists in the text itself, yes, but not there alone. Through repetition and study—through years of performing the rites, building connections, and letting them settle into your bones—the text becomes a part of you. As an initiate, this is your most important task. It's bigger than memorization. It takes repetition and intention. Learning the ins and outs of circle and the hows and whys of your traditional practice may begin with memorization, but it takes time and consistency to really internalize them. When your elders talk about *knowing* the rites, this is what they mean.

So know the rites. Read the material that's passed to you. Read it repeatedly. Then *do* it. Make it a part of you. When you struggle with where to go and where to focus or when you don't know what comes next, go back to your tradition's Book of Shadows. Annotate it. Criticize it. Copy it. Build connections from piece to piece. Figure out where those pieces came from and who put them there. Try to determine why it is the way it is. Make it yours. In those moments when you forget the words while everyone is counting on you (because you will have those moments), your *understanding* of the material will transcend the script and you'll be able to work your magic regardless. With that growing understanding, you may also find that your retention improves dramatically. Memorization is much easier when you know the purpose behind what you're performing.

Beyond memorizing rituals, every tradition has its own oral lore, protocol, and histories. As a new initiate, your best bet is often to shut your mouth and really focus on listening. A great deal of what you'll learn won't come from circling formally with your coven. Instead, it will happen at the dinner table before ritual, sitting around and laughing over a beer, trading stories and experiences while just hanging out, or during late-night phone conversations in between meetings. But you need to listen and watch carefully. Take advantage of the elders in your sphere. It won't be long before no one is left alive to talk about Wicca's heydays in the latter half of the twentieth century. These are our histories, and it's our duty to preserve them. Ask questions, ask for stories, ask for other perspectives, and then listen attentively.

Finally, continue to read. We live in an age when information can be had in mere minutes with access to a computer or a public library. There's no excuse not to have a basic grasp of Wiccan history, particularly where it concerns your own tradition and your own upline. Who were the major players? What controversies have arisen? What were the most influential movements, books, and events? There have been many times in recent history when materials relevant to the study of Witchcraft, religion, the gods, and magic were very difficult to come by. When Wicca was first taking shape and drawing public attention, there were only a few popularly available books from which to choose. There was no internet—no easy way to contact others and get information. Witches relied on the handful of small newsletters in print, letters through the mail, and contact with local communities (if they were lucky enough to have them). Today, there are literally thousands of titles and hundreds of thousands of websites to choose from. You can go to major chain booksellers and buy Pagan magazines. Libraries have metaphysical sections, and interlibrary loan allows you to acquire most titles for free, even if your local library doesn't have what you need on hand. There are social media sites not just for traditional Wiccans as a whole (though there are plenty of those) but also for individual traditions and even individual states and towns. With so many resources available, there are very few legitimate excuses not to take advantage.

Not all Witches are scholars. As a new initiate, it's not your job to become a researcher, a theologian, a social scientist, or a literary critic. While it's true that, on the whole, contemporary Pagans and Witches of all types tend to be a bit more bookish than the general population, that's not a requirement for becoming a priestess or priest of the Wica. You won't read a certain number of books and then automatically become a magical adept with a direct channel to the divine. Reading is a tool like anything else. More central is the need to cultivate a sense of curiosity. As an initiate, continue to seek out what you don't yet know. Never stop. Learn your history. Seek out unfamiliar magical techniques. Absorb lessons from the people who've been on this path longer than you. Write them down or do whatever else you need to do to remember them. Don't just memorize—understand. Be modest about what you know, and humble about what you don't know. As long as you're curious, you'll never be bored.

 FROM THE CIRCLE

Many books on occult subjects and those that are deemed "occult classics" are today out of print or just not available. A practical solution to this challenge is easier than you think! Many bigger libraries run by counties or municipalities in the United States have a service available called interlibrary loan. Most of the older books that have been around for a while, especially the out-of-print ones, can be borrowed free of charge (at least at my local library) when your library is able to track down a copy for you. I frequently request books from my library and rarely are they unable to find it. My library only allows five books per person at a time, so I keep a list handy so that I may read at my own pace and time my requests.

—*Thorn Nightwind, priest of the*
Horsa and Sacred Pentagraph traditions

To Dare

The popular refrain in many Wiccan and open Pagan spaces is that the Craft is "whatever makes you comfortable" or "whatever makes you happy." We're told over and over again to listen to our intuition, to modify rituals and spells to accommodate our personal preferences, to choose magical tools and ingredients according to what we feel, and to throw out those things that we simply don't want to do or think about. We tell newcomers that there's nothing to be afraid of—Witchcraft is about liberation, coming into your personal power, and being who you truly are.

Well, pardon me, but all of those things are pretty terrifying if you really stop and think about them. The process of becoming free—of learning who you are and living in accordance with that, unapologetically—is nothing short of miraculous. It forces you to cast off relationships that are toxic. Your professional and personal lives are radically altered. You will begin to walk outside of what is usually considered to be socially acceptable. You will offend people. This is what people mean when they insist that Witches are scary. Witches are many things throughout history, depending on whom you talk to and where you look, but they are almost always frightening, and it's because they pose a threat to the status quo. Witchcraft is fundamentally transgressive. Witches are outsiders. Witches are boundary crossers. Sometimes they can be spotted, but other times they blend right in, which makes them that much scarier. They could be *anyone*. From both the inside and the outside, Witchcraft has the potential to be very, very unnerving. Realizing your own power, touching the gods and spirits, working magic, and moving through the world having glimpsed those things beyond what people normally see is at times frightening.

There are many ways to be a Wiccan, and many more ways to be a Witch, but one thing that is consistently true is this: effective Witchcraft is uncomfortable. Your Craft should challenge you. It should push you to do things beyond what you already know you can do. It should break down barriers. It should change your thinking. It should change the way you walk in the world. If you insist on avoiding those things that force you to reconsider yourself and your world—if you only focus on those happy things that come easiest—then your Witchcraft will be impotent and ultimately meaningless.

If we only ever put ourselves in positions where we're comfortable, we don't give ourselves the opportunity to learn or experience anything new.

I'm not necessarily advocating completely tossing out personal boundaries, exposing ourselves to unhealthy or risky situations just for the sake of it, or going along with something that scares us because we're worried that if we don't we're not "real Witches" or something equally absurd. We are each in charge of deciding where our own boundaries lie. You still get to be the final authority in what is and isn't appropriate for you, and you can take things as slowly as you wish. But if you always turn away from those things that challenge you, how will you grow?

Traditional Wicca is not about sticking to "what makes you comfortable." You don't get to just change or throw out those things that you don't like simply because they "don't feel right." If something doesn't feel right, ask yourself why. Question what you're being taught, certainly. Argue, explore, and figure out what works best for you. Experiment and figure out effective alternatives. Allow for the possibility that what "doesn't feel right" might be the result of your own personal baggage or misguided thinking—things that you need to cast off. Whatever you decide in the end, do so with self-awareness and intention. But don't let the aim be comfort. This is the Witch cult—marked by midnight sabbats, secret rituals, and communion with the spirits of the underworld—not a hotel vacation or an evening spent snuggling with your favorite blanket. If you feel safe and comfortable all the time, that's a hint that something is going wrong.

Before we can begin processing our discomfort and growing our practice, we must first confront it. In my years of practice, I find that one of the scariest things for Witches trying something new is the prospect of getting things wrong. We put off rituals, magical projects, necessary conversations, and new explorations because... why? The timing isn't right. We don't have the space we want. We don't have the supplies we think we need. We don't have enough free time. We're tired. It was a tough workweek. We feel weird doing it alone instead of with a group. We don't feel right doing it in a group and would rather be alone. We've never done this before and we might get it wrong.

It's easy to come up with reasons to not do things. Sometimes, those reasons are legitimate. Everyone is busy. I get it. I come home from work some days and I barely have the energy for much more than lying on my couch and binge-watching a favorite TV show. Sometimes, I really have to psych myself up for coven meetings. Work drains me. Spending ten minutes in front of my bedroom altar talking to my gods feels like one more chore that I just can't handle. And the fact that I feel that way sometimes makes me feel even worse. Add kids, spouses, illnesses, and other responsibilities into the mix and things get even more challenging.

But a lot of the time we're just making excuses, and we know it.

Things will never be ideal. The perfect moment isn't coming. You may never have everything you need. You may never feel completely confident and assured of your success. So do whatever it is that you're putting off regardless. Understand that it won't be perfect. Part of being brave means knowing that you could fail—that things won't go according to plan—and doing it anyway.

Witchcraft is many things to many people, but one thing it should always be is challenging. Don't throw things out just because they're hard. Don't overlook important lessons just because they push you out of your comfort zone. Don't succumb to fear or excuses.

FROM THE CIRCLE

When you have moments of fear and panic, consider them, weigh them, chew on them. Most of the time, when my gut has said run, I've run, and it's been because I was in a dangerous situation, so it all worked out well. But sometimes my gut says, "Run—no—stay—no—I don't know! Shit!" When this happens, it's usually because I'm being challenged at a very fundamental level. Becoming Pagan and then seeking with a traditional coven fundamentally changed the direction of my life and the people in it, and it was a massive shift. It was *not* a thing lightly taken. No amount of divination was going to give me the "right" answer. No amount of consultation with my husband, friends, or high priestess and high priest was going to tell me what to do. I had to decide if the risk was worth the potential rewards and act on my own best judgment, knowing this would change my life and the lives of everyone I loved in a very real and significant way. Scary, right? That kind of soul-searching is the hardest part, but was among the most amazing and fruitful moments of my life, on par with marrying my husband and the birth of my son. It was that profound. And like those events, it has rippled out in an amazing and beautiful way into all aspects of my life.

—Wren, first degree priestess

To Will

There are an awful lot of things in life that are completely out of our control. Maybe most things. Where we're born and how we grow up are out of our hands, yet they say a lot about the opportunities that we'll have as adults. We also don't get to choose our own bodies, and these limit us just as strictly. On top of all that, sometimes things just happen to us. With billions of people in the world just trying to get by, we're bound to crash into each other from time to time, and sometimes these encounters leave us reeling. Many religions seek to explain or justify life's many disparities. Humans have wrestled with the problems of evil and suffering throughout history and our solutions usually leave us wanting. Sadly, Wiccan solutions are usually no exception. The truth is Wicca tends to focus on the here and now rather than those larger, vexing questions that usually require more elaborate, dogmatic cosmologies. As a community, we're not great at explaining why bad things happen to good people or what everything all means in the end. Those conversations are left to your more intimate coven communities, informed by your unique experiences and according to your own needs and circumstances. It takes a lot of hubris to say definitively to another person why it is that they suffer, and the prospect (I hope) makes most Wiccans uncomfortable. Individually, we may hold any number of different beliefs about those things beyond our power. They nonetheless remain beyond our power.

But there are many things that *are* within our control.

There are a lot of people in the world who don't take responsibility for themselves and their actions, and then they wonder why life doesn't go the way they want. They blame others when things go wrong, or they sit by and let opportunity pass them by because they're afraid to pursue it.

As an initiate of the Wica, you are both a magician and a priest or priestess of the gods. Part of coming into your own as a Witch means learning to exercise your Will, capital *W*. This isn't simply what you want (though that may be part of it); it's what we might think of as our life's purpose. It's those things that are required of you to fulfill that purpose, those things that further you on your path to becoming what you're supposed to be. Some ceremonial magicians and practitioners of other traditions within the Western mystery schools speak of "ascension" or "climbing the Tree of Life," to use more Qabalistic terms. Some Wiccans believe that we reincarnate for the sake of learning lessons. Your Will is the intent behind those actions that move you forward, whatever terms you choose to use.

You may not be sure about your life's purpose, or even believe that there is such a thing, but as a new initiate it's time to really take control of those things that impact the sort of person you wish to become. This is way less esoteric than it usually sounds. Personally, I think of things this way: Am I doing everything I possibly can to live a good life?

A "good life" isn't easy to define, either, but I find that we usually know when we're getting it wrong. Are you making choices that are destructive? Are you hurting yourself by not addressing something you need to? Are you not doing something you should because you're lazy or afraid? Do you really have control over your own life or do you allow others to make your decisions for you?

There's plenty that's beyond our control, but now's the time to take charge of everything else. Take your self-care seriously. Cultivate self-awareness. Do good work. Be sincere. Be conscious of how you treat others. Develop foresight and move through the world thoughtfully. When you feel compelled to complain about something, consider what you can do to change things for the better. Be an instigator.

Initiates occupy a place of power and the position demands respect. You're a priest and a Witch. Make sure you're acting like it.

To Be Silent

After all the work that goes into outer court, it's tempting to breathe a sigh of relief and forget that things are really only just beginning. Out in the wider community, even in spaces where most people are solitary practitioners, we often talk about *initiates* as though they're automatically wiser, more qualified, or more magical than other kinds of Witches. Hopefully by now you understand that this isn't actually the case, but the stereotype persists. Initiation is important in traditional Wicca, certainly, but all it means for sure is that the person has been accepted as a member. It doesn't mean that person is automatically qualified to be a teacher, or that she's an expert, or that her magic is more effective, or that she warrants more respect than someone from another tradition that does things a bit differently. Initiation is many things, but it's never a guarantee of wisdom or experience.

As a new initiate, you are a beginner. It may not feel that way—you may have been practicing for years, busting your butt to get where you are—but you're really only on the verge of something. Now is the time to study, to listen, to reflect, and to learn. If you're talking, you're not listening. If you're on the internet running your mouth about things you don't yet understand, you're using up valuable time that you could be using to actually practice Witchcraft.

Every coven will have its own policy about interacting with wider communities.[21] Your high priestess and high priest may ask their initiates to abstain completely from talking about Craft-related subjects in public places (particularly online). They may also ask that you not participate in open Pagan or magical communities, at least at first. These kinds of requests are not designed to confine you or stifle your explorations. They're intended to encourage focus, to prevent confusion, and to protect coven or tradition secrets. Brand-new first degrees often have difficulty appreciating when to share and when to keep something private. A focused period of relative solitude is extremely beneficial. Initiation can be disorienting, and, further, it's a challenge to keep those private things to yourself. You *want* people to know what's changed for you. You *want* to share your excitement. You *want* to correct people who may have misconceptions about what you do. And there are certainly plenty of things you *can* share. There's a lot you *can* talk about. But silence is often the better choice, particularly when dealing with strangers in public places.

Learn to be silent.

Learn to keep private thoughts private.

Keep other people's business off the internet.

If you're not sure if you should or shouldn't share, err on the side of shouldn't. You can always change your mind later, after you've gotten some feedback from others in your coven. If you've taken an oath of secrecy (and you probably have), remember that it can be just as revealing to deny something as it is to confirm it. Learn to leave the overly curious or the ignorant guessing. Telling them that you *don't* do something or that something *isn't* true can be just as compromis-

---

21. And they should share this policy with you upfront; it shouldn't be a surprise saved for the day after your initiation, leaving you feeling manipulated and cut off from communities that may be important to you.

ing to your oath as sharing what you *do*. Negotiating this type of verbal sleight of hand requires a great deal of reserve and finesse. Begin practicing now.

 FROM THE CIRCLE

Initiation was a challenge because there was a lot I couldn't discuss with my spouse, so it was a leap of faith for both of us. He knew that I had discussed with my high priestess that my marriage was my first vow and that I wouldn't do anything to violate it, but beyond that, he just had to trust me *and* my high priestess and high priest. I spend a lot of time checking in with him when working out schedules for circle and talking to him about my covenmates (and he's met all of them *and* their spouses and children, who are mostly also non-Pagan). It's an ongoing thing, but it's been a whole new phase of our marriage. One that's been really challenging, for sure, but it's also made us stronger for it.

—*Wren, first degree priestess*

Too many of us are in too much of a hurry to be elders. Every stage of Craft practice comes with its own lessons and is valuable for exactly what it is. As a new initiate, your job is to learn your Craft, to build relationships with your covenmates, and to explore what it means to connect with the gods. Your job is not to correct strangers on the internet, to lord your new title over anyone else, or to teach would-be Witches because suddenly you feel so qualified. Do not try to rush through this. Bad first degrees make bad second degrees make bad third degrees. Be the best first degree you can. Be the best beginner you can. This is one of the most exciting periods in Craft training, and you'll never have it again.

Use this time to absorb the experience of the people around you. When your high priestess tells stories about the people who make up your upline, pay attention. When your covenmates share their personal magical pursuits, their own difficulties, and their own revelations, pay attention. Shut your own mouth, put away the keyboard, and listen. It's amazing what you'll learn in these early days, and you'll learn even more when you come to appreciate that you're still a beginner.

Keep these four pillars in mind and enjoy the ride. Be diligent. Be curious. Be brave. Be discerning. This is a lifelong process, and there's no endpoint. Welcome to the family!

MAY THE GODS PRESERVE THE CRAFT

Night is well settled over the city, and the sounds of contented laughter mingle with crickets, the humming of distant streetlamps, and cars passing through the intersection at the top of the hill. If you didn't know better, you would swear you were passing out of some enchanted land—through a portal in the middle of a major city, frequented only by the few residents with the magical sense to find it. But that boundary is an illusion. That sense of enchantment is potentially anywhere, so long as you have the inclination to discover it. And we are Witches, after all.

The rite is over, but this circle is unbroken. It spirals back, connecting with thousands of circles cast by as many Witches. In secret wooded patches nestled between city streets, in sprawling fields, in public parks and the basements of rented buildings, in cramped living rooms ... our circle touches them all.

The last vestiges of smoke rise from the cauldron, the charcoals burnt to little more than ash. The candles are melted down in their holders, wax hardening on the altar, translucent droplets on the hilt of the sword. Libations have been poured, stories have been shared, and the gods have been invoked. The Wheel turns again, back to the past but also toward the future.

Epilogue

I hope that you've enjoyed this book, and that you've found it to be informative. Many people are surprised that traditional forms of Wicca continue to survive, let alone that they are growing, diversifying, and strengthening in an era marked by almost overwhelming magical and religious variety. Though so much has changed about the world since the inception of Wicca, it continues to call new initiates. Healthy covens sprout in unlikely places, led by Witches of all ages, with myriad backgrounds. If you have felt that call, then I hope I've been able to help you find better footing on the path.

FURTHER READING

The following books are valuable to seekers of traditional Wicca, regardless of which traditions interest you. Some are by historians, tracing the history of Witchcraft in a particular region. Others are by practitioners, designed to help expand your magical knowledge. Still others are biographies of important figures in Wicca's history, which will provide you with additional insight into its contemporary development and hopefully inspire your own practice.

Aburrow, Yvonne. *All Acts of Love & Pleasure: Inclusive Wicca.* Glastonbury: Avalonia, 2014.
In this important book, Aburrow tackles the subject of inclusivity in initiatory Wicca. How does Wicca speak to practitioners with varied needs and from varied backgrounds? Though it has received a great deal of attention for its discussion of gender binaries and sexuality, this work contains so much more and is absolutely worth considering regardless of your own experience or tradition.

Aradia, Lady Sable. *The Witch's Eight Paths of Power: A Complete Course in Magick and Witchcraft.* San Francisco: Red Wheel/ Weiser, 2014.
A lot of books about magic and ritual instruct practitioners to "raise energy," but what exactly does that mean? Aradia explores an assortment

of techniques in detail, any of which may be used to lend power to your own magical practice.

Bado, Nikki. *Coming to the Edge of the Circle: A Wiccan Initiation Ritual.* **New York: Oxford University, 2012.**
Religion scholar and Wiccan priestess Nikki Bado analyzes the role of initiation in Wicca, from the unusual perspective of someone wearing the hats of both an insider and an outsider. This book is valuable for considering the how and why of initiatory experiences, regardless of your specific tradition.

Bourne, Lois. *Dancing with Witches.* **London: Robert Hale Limited, 1998.**
Lois Bourne was part of Gerald Gardner's Bricket Wood coven. As a longtime practitioner and friend of Gardner, Bourne's works are full of interesting anecdotes and a perspective that only comes from decades of experience.

Bracelin, Jack. *Gerald Gardner: Witch.* **Thame, UK: I-H-O Books, 1999.**
Originally published in 1960, this biography is the combined effort of Jack Bracelin and Idries Shah. Though it can feel a little disjointed, this book is full of worthwhile stories about Wicca's famous founder.

Buckland, Raymond. *Witchcraft from the Inside: Origins of the Fastest Growing Religious Movement in America.* **St. Paul, MN: Llewellyn, 2001.**
Ray Buckland was a prolific Wiccan author and one of the people responsible for the spread of Wicca to the United States. He also gets credit for the development of solitary Wicca. Here is his own history of the movement, written from the perspective of an insider.

Clifton, Chas S. *Her Hidden Children: The Rise of Wicca and Paganism in America*. Lanham, MD: AltaMira, 2006.

A prominent scholar of contemporary Pagan studies, Clifton looks specifically at the development of Wicca and Paganism in the United States. This relatively short history is both thorough and unintimidating.

Cochrane, Robert, with Evan John Jones. *The Robert Cochrane Letters*. Edited by Michael Howard. Somerset, UK: Capall Bann Publishing, 2002.

Cochrane's writing is intentionally cryptic, but these short letters are responsible for the development of much of what we call "traditional Witchcraft" today. That alone would make them worth reading, but they are of particular interest to Wiccans because of Cochrane's criticism of Gardner's version of the Craft.

Crowther, Patricia. *High Priestess: The Life & Times of Patricia Crowther*. Blaine, WA: Phoenix Publishing, 1998.

Like Ray Buckland, Patricia Crowther is a prolific writer and a prominent leader of the early Craft. This is her autobiography (actually, it's one of several autobiographies), and it's full of personal accounts spanning Wiccan history.

Davies, Morganna, and Aradia Lynch. *Keepers of the Flame: Interviews with Elders of Traditional Witchcraft in America*. Providence, RI: Olympian Press, 2001.

This book is a collection of personal stories from experienced Witches, several of whom have been at this since before I was even born. These interviews are full of insight and represent several traditions.

Farrar, Janet, and Gavin Bone. *Lifting the Veil: A Witches' Guide to Trance-Prophesy, Drawing Down the Moon, and Ecstatic Ritual.* **Portland, OR: Acorn Guild Press, 2016.**

In this book, Farrar and Bone explore the ritual of drawing down the moon, one of Wicca's central rites, as well as other modes of direct communion with the divine. Farrar and Bone have both made enormous contributions to Wicca, and this text is of particular interest to traditional practitioners.

Farrar, Stewart. *What Witches Do.* **Blaine, WA: Phoenix Publishing, 1991.**

Farrar wrote this book as a young journalist, exploring Wicca as an outsider, before his eventual initiation. This is still my favorite book for depicting the inner workings of a coven, even today, and my students have found it to be one of the more useful books I recommend.

Filan, Kenaz, and Raven Kaldera. *Drawing Down the Spirits: The Traditions and Techniques of Spirit Possession.* **Rochester, VT: Destiny Books, 2009.**

Filan and Kaldera explore the mechanics of working with the gods directly through possession. This book is not specific to any one tradition, and it will prove useful for those curious about the many ways we interact with gods and spirits.

Fitch, Ed. *A Grimoire of Shadows: Witchcraft, Paganism & Magick.* **St. Paul, MN: Llewellyn, 1997.**

Full of rituals, poetry, and decades of experience, Ed Fitch's book is a classic in the wider Pagan community. There's a good chance you've encountered Fitch's work at open events or online and just never realized it.

Fitch, Eric. *In Search of Herne the Hunter.* **Berks, UK: Capall Bann Publishing, 1994.**

Despite the title, Fitch's book is a solid introduction to horned gods in general, not just Herne. Relatively short and full of interesting lore and histories, this book is worthwhile for Wiccans of all flavors.

Gaiman, Neil. *American Gods.* **New York: HarperCollins, 2001.**

Although this book is a work of fiction, Gaiman raises a number of challenging questions worth discussing. What happens to old gods in a new land with new people? How does social change give rise to new gods? This is one of very few books that I actually require my own outer court students to read.

Gardner, Gerald. *The Meaning of Witchcraft.* **York Beach, ME: Red Wheel/Weiser, 2004.**

Many covens include this book in their reading lists for seekers, including my own. No matter the tradition you pursue, it's likely that you'll be asked to read this at some point. However you feel about Gardner, his contributions to the contemporary Witchcraft movement cannot be overstated, and a comprehensive study of the Craft demands that we read his work.

Hanna, Jon. *What Thou Wilt: Traditional and Innovative Trends in Post-Gardnerian Witchcraft.* **Westport, Ireland: Evertype, 2010.**

Hanna wrote this book as part of his own Wiccan training. He discusses the differences between traditional and eclectic (what he calls "innovative") forms of Wicca in a thoughtful, accessible way that will appeal to both confused beginners and more experienced Witches looking for a nuanced perspective.

Heselton, Philip. *Doreen Valiente Witch*. Woodbury, MN: Llewellyn, 2016.

Doreen Valiente had more of an impact on the contemporary Witchcraft movement than almost anyone, and here Heselton details her life, both inside and outside the Craft. Heselton tells a good story and isn't afraid to insert his own theories, which makes for an engaging, well-researched read.

Heselton, Philip. *Witchfather: A Life of Gerald Gardner* (Volumes 1 and 2). Loughborough, UK: Thoth Publications, 2012.

This is the most complete biography of Gerald Gardner available, from one of Wicca's most knowledgeable writers. Heselton has a knack for capturing the humanity of his subjects, reminding us that behind any religious movement are the visions and quirks of people just living their lives.

Hutton, Ronald. *The Triumph of the Moon: A History of Modern Pagan Witchcraft*. New York: Oxford University Press, 1999.

This is, hands down, the most thorough history of Wicca and neighboring Witchcraft and Pagan traditions currently available. If you're unaccustomed to academic writing, you may find Hutton somewhat dry at times, but this book is well worth the effort.

Lamond, Frederic. *Fifty Years of Wicca*. Sutton Mallet, UK: Green Magic, 2004.

Frederic Lamond was a member of one of Wicca's earliest covens and he's full of (sometimes unflattering) stories about the colorful people at the head of Wicca's development.

Leland, Charles. *Aradia or the Gospel of Witches*. Translated by Mario Pazzaglini and Dina Pazzaglini. Blaine, WA: Phoenix Publishing, 1998.

This short text is one of the most frequently cited by Witchcraft practitioners in any tradition. It inspired early Wiccans and continues to be a cornerstone of many types of modern Witchcraft. This edition is my favorite because of the useful insights provided by the Pazzaglinis.

Lipp, Deborah. *The Elements of Ritual: Air, Fire, Water & Earth in the Wiccan Circle*. St. Paul, MN: Llewellyn, 2003.

Wiccan ritual can be quite elaborate, and it's important to understand why we do what we do. Lipp breaks things down step-by-step, lending context to the words and actions that many of us take for granted.

Lloyd, Michael G. *Bull of Heaven: The Mythic Life of Eddie Buczynski and the Rise of the New York Pagan*. Hubbardston, MA: Asphodel Press, 2012.

This is so much more than a biography of Eddie Buczynski, the Wiccan high priest famous for his role in founding the Minoan Brotherhood and Welsh Traditional Witchcraft. This is a history of the New York Pagan scene in the last quarter of the twentieth century, worth reading regardless of your own tradition.

Murray, Margaret. *The Witch-Cult in Western Europe: A Study in Anthropology*. London: Oxford University Press, 1963.

One of the early classics of contemporary Witchcraft, this book is still worth reading in light of the incredible impact it had on the magical world. Murray was an Egyptologist and folklorist, and now we know her history to be suspect, but she remains important. She's not the easiest to read thanks to the time period and her dry style, but it's worthwhile to make the effort.

Pratchett, Terry. *Small Gods.* **New York: HarperCollins, 1992.**
A work of fiction from one of the fantasy's most beloved authors, *Small Gods* is a humorous, surprisingly thought-provoking introduction to polytheism. Useful for thinking about power, origins, and what it means to be a devotee in a fun, approachable way.

Sanders, Maxine. *Fire Child: The Life and Magic of Maxine Sanders 'Witch Queen.'* **Oxford, UK: Mandrake of Oxford, 2008.**
This is the autobiography of high priestess Maxine Sanders, famous for her role in the development of Alexandrian Wicca and for her marriage to "King of the Witches" Alex Sanders. Maxine Sanders has led a fascinating life, and this book makes for an informative read, particularly if you feel drawn to Alexandrian Wicca.

Sylvan, Dianne. *The Circle Within: Creating a Wiccan Spiritual Tradition.* **St. Paul, MN: Llewellyn, 2003.**
Appropriate for all types of Wiccan practitioners, Sylvan's book helps readers develop a meaningful daily practice regardless of their experience level or personal situation. I reread this book every couple of years and always find something worth remembering.

Valiente, Doreen. *Witchcraft for Tomorrow.* **Blaine, WA: Phoenix Publishing, 1978.**
Often called the mother of modern Witchcraft, Valiente's lyrical writing style and incredible experiences make her a must-read for all Wiccans. Many of her books cover similar materials, and this one is my favorite as an introduction to the Craft.

ABOUT THE CONTRIBUTORS

Ari Mankey is a third degree Gardnerian high priestess and a devotee of Aphrodite, and she has practiced the Craft for over twenty years. Away from the circle she works as a mad scientist in Palo Alto, California. She likes her coffee with cream and her beer as black as her soul.

Acacia identifies as an animist and polytheist, and she is currently approaching her second year as a student in a traditional outer court. She is a jeweler and lapidary who runs her own business. You can see her art at www.lapidify.net.

Corvus is a Wiccan initiate from Michigan's Upper Peninsula. She's run open circles and led community workshops for more than a decade. When she's not in circle, she's cosplaying characters from her favorite fandoms, crocheting something awesome, or talking to one of her two cats, Izzy and Topaz. Oh yeah, or her husband.

Deb Snavely is a traditional elder who founded Gardnerian covens in both Oregon and Washington. A presenter at a few early Panthea-Cons, she was editor of *Pagan Muse & World Report* from 1993 to 1997. Now she contributes articles on traditional Wicca and Witchcraft to international online magazines *The Wiccan* and *Wiccan Rede Online*. She has also served as volunteer director of the now-defunct Bay Area Pagan Assemblies (BAPA). Deb currently volunteers as an officer of the New Wiccan Church, International, which you can visit at www.newwiccanchurch.org.

Jason Mankey is a Pagan blogger, a columnist for *Witches & Pagans*, and the managing editor of the Pagan Portal on Patheos. He talks about rock and roll, Pagan deities, and various aspects of Pagan history at festivals across North America. Find him online at www.patheos.com/blogs/panmankey.

Lukaos is a third degree high priest who enjoys collecting and telling stories about the past. He has a lovingly neglected website at www.geraldgardner.com.

Liam has been practicing for around eighteen years or so. He's a third degree high priest. Married to his high priestess, he and his wife have two daughters. Liam graduated from Sullivan University and is an Army veteran. He practices biodynamic gardening, is a runner, and loves primitive archery.

Phoenix LeFae is equal parts blue-eyed wanderer and passionate devotee of the Goddess. She attended her first Reclaiming ritual in 1995, and she's been hooked ever since. An initiate in Reclaiming, the Avalon Druid Order, and Gardnerian Wicca, Phoenix has had the pleasure of teaching and leading ritual globally. Find out more at her shop Milk & Honey (www.Milk-and-Honey.com).

Rayn is a Gardnerian high priestess running a coven in Chattanooga, Tennessee. She can be contacted through Witchvox for those seekers called to the Olde Ways. May the gods guide you on your path.

Thorn Nightwind is a priest and Witch in the Horsa tradition and Sacred Pentagraph tradition. He loves midnight bonfires with friends, working with herbs and plants, and nature walks in the woods. He enjoys the study of Witchcraft and esoteric lore in all its many forms.

Wren is a first degree Wiccan, academic, artist, wife, and mother.

To Write to the Author

If you wish to contact the author or would like more information about this book, please write to the author in care of Llewellyn Worldwide Ltd. and we will forward your request. Both the author and the publisher appreciate hearing from you and learning of your enjoyment of this book and how it has helped you. Llewellyn Worldwide Ltd. cannot guarantee that every letter written to the author can be answered, but all will be forwarded. Please write to:

Thorn Mooney
⅟ Llewellyn Worldwide
2143 Wooddale Drive
Woodbury, MN 55125-2989
Please enclose a self-addressed stamped envelope for reply,
or $1.00 to cover costs. If outside the U.S.A., enclose
an international postal reply coupon.

Many of Llewellyn's authors have websites with additional information and resources. For more information, please visit our website at http://www.llewellyn.com.